The African-American Experience

Ray Spangenburg and Diane K. Moser

Facts On File, Inc.

American Historic Places: *The African-American Experience*
Copyright © 1997 by Ray Spangenburg and Diane K. Moser

Facts On File, Inc.
11 Penn Plaza
New York NY 10001

Library of Congress Cataloging–in–Publication Data

Spangenberg, Ray, 1939.
    American historic places : the African-American experience / by
Ray Spangenburg and Diane K. Moser.
        p.   cm.
    Includes bibliographical references and index.
    Summary: Explores ten locations that have had significant impact
on the African-American experience.
    ISBN 0-8160-3400-1
    1. Afro-Americans—History—Juvenile literature.   2. Historic
sites—United States—Juvenile literature.   [1. Afro-Americans—
History. 2. Historic sites.]   I. Moser, Diane, 1944-   .
II.Title.
E185.S598   1996
973′. 0496—dc20   96-27992
                                                                              CIP

Text design by Cathy Rincon
Cover design by Dorothy Wachtenheim
Illustrations pages viii, 13, 64, 74, 82, 120 by Jeremy Eagle

This book is printed on acid-free paper.

Printed in the United States of America

RRD/INNO 10 9 8 7 6 5 4 3 2 1

CONTENTS

For Lorrie, Buzz

and all the Freedom Marchers

at Birmingham and Decatur

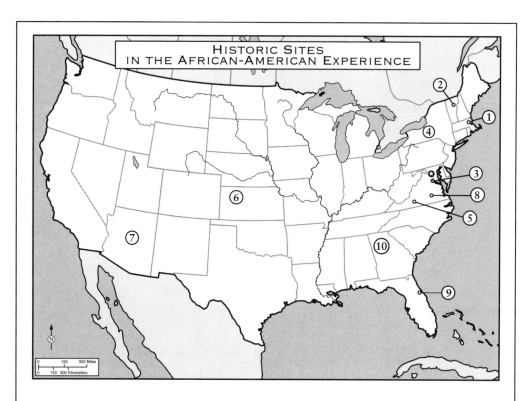

HISTORIC SITES IN THE AFRICAN-AMERICAN EXPERIENCE

1   The African Meeting House: the oldest existing African-American church

2   The Old Stone House: academy built by educator Alexander Lucius Twilight

3   Cedar Hill: home of freedom fighter Frederick Douglass

4   Home of Harriet Tubman: house of an Underground Railroad conductor

5   Booker T. Washington National Monument: birthplace of an educator

6   Nicodemus Historic District: town built by Exoduster Movement

7   Fort Verde, Arizona: station of Buffalo Soldiers in the West

8   Maggie Lena Walker Historic District: home of the first female bank president

9   Mary McLeod Bethune House: home of an educator and activist

10 Martin Luther King, Jr., National Site: home of a great human rights leader

PREFACE TO THE SERIES

History doesn't have to be dry or stuffy. And it isn't exclusively about military skirmishes and legislative proclamations—they make up only a small part of it. History is the story of life events that happened to people who cared as passionately about their lives as we care about ours. And it's the story of events that often continue to shape and influence our lives today. But getting to the human side of these stories isn't always easy. That's why there's nothing like visiting the place where an event actually occurred to get the feel of what it all meant.

The study of historic places—what happened at a particular site and how the lives of the people there were affected—has emerged as a great way to approach history, to "relive" the experience and open up to the immense diversity of American culture. Every community and region is rich in such places—places that highlight real stories about real people and events. Even if you can't actually visit such a place, the next best thing is to go there through pictures and words. Use this book and the other books in this series as jumping-off points and look around your community for places where you can experience the world of the people who once lived in your own region—and begin exploring!

♦ ♦ ♦

Each volume in this series explores a different aspect of U.S. history by focusing on a few select places. This book takes a look at historic places in the United States associated with the experience of African Americans, from capture and enslavement in Africa through the continuing struggle for civil rights. Of course, choosing exactly which places to focus on in each book was one of the most difficult tasks of this project. We limited our choices to sites that had either been restored or maintained in authentic historic condition—most are National Historic Landmarks, chosen by the U.S. governent to be preserved for their historic significance. We also tried to include examples from a wide variety of locations, events and experiences, types of sites and time periods. We then limited our selections to just a few. But many other fascinating places exist throughout the country, and that's why we mentioned other related sites at the end of some chapters (under Exploring Further) and added a list of additional sites at the back of the book (More Places to Visit).

Each chapter begins with information about the site (At a Glance). Then we explore the place—what it's like and who lived there, how the place related to that person's life and work, and what it's like to visit there today. We also look closely at one feature of the site in "A Close-Up" section, followed by a section recapping how the site came to be a protected historic site (Preserving It for the Future). A list of books and other resources concludes each chapter (Exploring Further), directing readers to either a broader or closer view of the African-American experience in the United States.

Exploring historic sites not only provides a way to experience past events with fresh vividness and immediacy, it also offers a way of seeing the past through new eyes, through the eyes of those who lived it. For this adventure—and it can prove to be a lifetime adventure—this series will have accomplished its purpose if it provides the springboard for future explorations. In the words of an old Gaelic greeting, "May the wind be always at your back and may the road rise up to meet you," as you travel down these avenues of historical experience.

ACKNOWLEDGMENTS

So many people have helped with this book, we almost can't begin to count. Our appreciation to them all, including Pauline Copes Johnson, great-grand niece of Harriet Tubman and tour guide at the Harriet Tubman House, for taking the time to talk with us about the house and grounds where Tubman lived at the end of her life; Angela Bates Tompkins of the Nicodemus Society, for her efficient helpfulness in supplying information about the Exoduster movement and photos of the town of Nicodemus, Kansas; Akeema King, Jada Wilson, Jean Fives and Catherine Kershaw of Bethune-Cookman College for taking time to talk about Mary McLeod Bethune and the house in Florida where she lived; Park Rangers Celia Suggs at the Maggie L. Walker National Historic Site and Terri Leverton at Fort Verde for great research assistance; and Tracy Martin for her enthusiasm and helpfulness regarding the Old Stone House. And at Facts On File, our special thanks to Emily Spectre, for deftly handling the daunting production challenges of this series; to Nicole Bowen for her sharp eyes and keen intelligence and to James Warren, who helped us conceptualize the series.

INTRODUCTION

M ost people don't know the part played by African Americans in the earliest history of what Europeans called the New World. Two black explorers were among the first from the Old World to come to the North American continent—one, Estevanico, with a Spanish expedition, the other, Mathieu da Costa, as a guide for Samuel de Champlain in the North. Both preceded the arrival of Columbus whose expeditions included several Africans. The pilot of the *Santa Maria*, Pedro Alonzo Niño, has been identified as a black man.

Africans participated with Hernán Cortés in Mexico, Francisco Pizarro in Peru and Pedro de Alvarado in Quito. Thirty black men were with Vasco Núñez de Balboa when he first sighted the Pacific Ocean, and Africans accompanied Hernán de Alarcón and Francisco Vásquez de Coronado in New Mexico, while the aforementioned Estevanico opened up New Mexico and Arizona for Spain.

Jean-Baptiste Pointe du Sable, a black Frenchman, founded what became the city of Chicago, constructing the first building on that site.

In 1619, however, an event occurred that changed forever the course of American history and left an indelible blot on the times. A ship landed at the English colony of Jamestown, Virginia, with 20 Africans onboard. They had been carried as cargo and were sold to the colonists. The ship's captain was paid for the Africans' passage by colonists, who in turn required them to work off their debt as indentured servants, after which they became free. Later many owned land alongside their English neighbors.

Those who were brought from Africa on later ships endured an even worse fate. Captured in Africa, they were sold there to slave traders, who usually forced them to withstand a period of "conditioning" to slavery before leaving African shores. Then, loaded like ship cargo, they endured an arduous "middle passage" across the Atlantic Ocean, chained side by side in the cramped cargo hold below deck. Many became ill and died; some went insane from confinement. Those who arrived in the New World often underwent another period of training, usually in Jamaica, in preparation for the jobs and attitudes that would be required of them as slaves. Finally, shiploads of human beings were brought to the Eastern colonial ports and sold off like cattle. The slaves were considered property, with no rights. Many tasks, especially in the farm fields, were managed by overseers with ready whips, who punished severely those who stepped out of line. Education was forbidden. Slaves typically lived in huts and suffered arduous lives, haunted by the caprice of those in power and, almost universally, without hope of escape, freedom or a better future.

By the early 1770s, slavery existed in every one of the 13 colonies, although conditions were more severe for slaves in the South than in the North. By the start of the Revolutionary War in 1776, more than 150 years of slavery had passed since the first 20 Africans arrived in Jamestown. Much of the new nation's economy was built on labor that was free, except for the cost of a handful of meals per day and a few scattered hovels. America was trapped in an ugly, inhumane tradition, contradicting the very causes of freedom and justice that the framers of the Declaration of Independence had written about so eloquently. Some African Americans lived free during the years of the Revolution, but most of the burgeoning black population were enslaved.

Many African Americans greeted the Declaration of Independence with hope that, once the onerous burdens of English government and taxation were thrown off by the colonies, the new government would provide freedom for them as well. Crispus Attucks, an African American in Boston, was killed participating in what became known as the Boston Massacre. Many blacks fought on the side of the Continental Army during the War for Independence, including two who crossed the Delaware with General George Washington.

Despite the intentions of some framers of the Declaration of Independence, the clause banning slavery that appeared in early versions was stricken from the final version under pressure from slave owners. It was a crippling blow to the cause of freedom. Those who fought against slavery succeeded only in winning the abolition of the slave trade in 1808, but the law was not enforced, and illegal importation of slaves continued long after.

During the early years of the 19th century, building up to the Civil War (1861–65), the issue of whether or not to abolish slavery became argued more and more angrily. A division began to develop between the Northern states, where a growing industrial economy became less and less dependent on slaves, and the Southern states, where an agricultural economy still needed slavery to survive. As the Industrial Revolution took hold in England, streamlining textile production, demand grew for cotton, and savvy Southern landowners began to raise cotton to meet the demand. A highly labor-intensive crop, more cotton production meant an even greater dependence on slave labor, and the bonds of African-American slaves grew even tighter.

Many slaves ran away to safety in the North, as Harriet Tubman did. Tubman, however, returned to the South over and over to free other slaves and bring them to safety—often using the series of hiding places, underground tunnels, and safe houses known as the Underground Railroad. Many runaway slaves were killed; others were recaptured by their owners. In 1850, Congress passed the Fugitive Slave Act, which stipulated that a slave remained the property of his or her owner, even in a free state. This act meant that the North was no longer safe.

Freed slaves began to speak out more and more frankly, as former slave Frederick Douglass did, in favor of abolition. A growing consciousness among Northern whites began to take hold, a consciousness of the injustice of slavery. And many more joined the ranks in the fight for abolition.

Northerners tried to limit slavery's growth by abolishing it in newly formed states, but they were forced into compromises over and over. Manufacturers in New York City and other ports depended on Southern trade, and, for economic and political reasons, the Northern states *needed* to keep the United States together. So when a group of 11 Southern states seceded from the Union and formed the Confederate States of America in 1860–61, President Abraham Lincoln was forced to make a move to bring them back into the Union. On April 12, 1861, when the Confederate forces fired on Fort Sumter in South Carolina, Lincoln declared war. Two years later, in 1863, he enacted the Emancipation Proclamation to free the slaves in the seceded states. His proclamation did not, however, free slaves in the border states that were loyal to the Union. Lincoln had no authority to do that, and some 800,000 African Americans remained enslaved in loyal Union states even after the historic proclamation. Ironically, African Americans were not even admitted into the Union army until well into the war. By the end of the war, however, 156,000 black troops had fought for the Union army in 39 major battles. Of those soldiers, 22 received the Congressional Medal of Honor. Additionally, 39,000 blacks served in the Union navy, and some 200,000 more volunteered for nonmilitary service.

After the war, the slaves were freed at last by the ratification of the 13th Amendment to the Constitution, which proclaimed, "Neither slavery nor involuntary servitude shall exist within the United States." It was the end of 250 years of slavery.

But the African-American struggle was not over. Free, but with no land to till and no place to go, many former slaves stayed on the same plantations, working as sharecroppers under conditions no better or even worse than before. Lincoln, who had developed plans for the Reconstruction period that followed the end of the war, was killed by an assassin's bullet in 1865. His successor, Andrew Johnson, was weak and unsure, and Southern whites attempted to return to the ways of the past. But Congress passed a Civil Rights Act in April 1866 that gave citizenship to former slaves, and in June 1866 Congress passed the 14th Amendment, which gave black men the right to vote. Then Congress forced the former Confederate states to ratify the amendment. African Americans had political power for the first time. Their vote put Republican Ulysses S. Grant in the presidency, and many blacks were elected to state legislatures, where they often learned to read and write on the job—which had been prohibited before.

But unrest ruled the South. Angry, defeated whites organized the Ku Klux Klan (KKK), a secret organization of white supremists who lynched, tarred and feathered, whipped, threatened and burned the homes of blacks who aroused their vengeance. The KKK intimidated blacks to keep them from voting in an attempt to put the Southern Democrats back into office—despite the majority's wishes.

In 1877, Rutherford B. Hayes, a candidate from Ohio who had fought in the Union army, needed votes for his presidential campaign. He ended the struggle in favor of Southern whites by giving in to their "states' rights" campaign. Southern whites contended that individual states should control their own affairs. Translated that meant the end of African-American progress and the establishment of the so-called Jim Crow laws in the South. Discrimination and segregation became law through Jim Crow, which was enabled by a series of Supreme Court decisions during the 1880s and 1890s. Throughout the South, separate facilities became the rule for everything from taxicab stands and drinking fountains to libraries and post offices. The Red Cross even kept segregated blood banks until the 1940s. Jim Crow laws remained in effect until they were challenged by civil rights activists in the 1960s.

Conditions in the South during Reconstruction and post-Reconstruction became so grim that a large number of blacks decided to leave, and a great migration took place. Many were drawn to northern industrial cities, where jobs seemed to beckon. Others, following the dream of having their own land, accepted the government invitation to become homesteaders in the 1870s and 1880s. They settled in the Midwest and Far West—often forming all-black communities such as Nicodemus, Kansas, or the towns of Boley, Langston and Summit in Oklahoma. Called Exodusters, more than 40,000 black sharecroppers in 1879 alone traveled to Kansas under the leadership of Benjamin "Pap" Singleton, many making the journey on foot.

Meanwhile, African-American leaders saw that education was the key that would ultimately open doors for poor blacks. Booker T. Washington, W. E. B. DuBois and Mary McLeod Bethune all made education available to young black people through the establishment of schools and colleges. While African-American leaders didn't all agree about the content and approach of the curriculum, they all saw that knowledge was power and served as role models to those who followed behind them.

In the 1920s the section of New York City called Harlem saw a brilliant flowering of the arts in the black community. Harlem was home to incomparable musician-composers such as Duke Ellington and W. C. Handy; singers such as Paul Robeson and Marian Anderson; writers such as poet

Langston Hughes and novelist Zora Neale Hurston; and performers such as actor Charles Gilpin and dancer Katharine Dunham. Through the sheer power and grace of their talent and the huge body of work, these men and women built a broad and strong foundation for African-American art.

Yet, when black soldiers returned home from World War I, having distinguished themselves by their courage, they were greeted by Ku Klux Klan lynchings and burnings. By the 1930s, racial tensions were high. The economic depression of those years caused unemployment throughout the country and increased the competition for the few jobs that existed. President Franklin Delano Roosevelt's New Deal did little at first to help blacks, until—under the influence of Mary McLeod Bethune and Eleanor Roosevelt—the programs began to be administered more fairly.

Yet through the 1940s the Jim Crow laws and "separate but equal" public schools—which were rarely equal—continued to be the rule of the day. Then on May 17, 1954, the U.S. Supreme Court, in a landmark decision known as *Brown* v. *the Board of Education*, outlawed racial segregation in the public schools. A second *Brown* v. *the Board of Education* decision followed on May 31, 1955, stipulating that educational integration was to be achieved with "all deliberate speed." And in a third milestone decision, the justices also placed a ban on segregation in tax-supported colleges and universities. In 1957, nine black teenagers tried to register at Central High School in Little Rock, Arkansas. The governor of Arkansas attempted to block their admittance, posting local National Guard units in front of the school to prevent them from entering. But the students did enter the school—under the protection of a special Supreme Court edict, a presidential proclamation and the protection of the 101st Army Airborne Division and a special federalized state militia. At last, after 80 years of Jim Crow laws, some real progress was afoot. In 1962, James Meredith enrolled as the first black student at the University of Mississippi. Others followed at various state universities across the South.

White southerners felt threatened; they believed that their way of life was at risk again. As long as former slaves were kept in a different social and economic class, whites could feel superior. For low-income whites this was especially important—they wanted to think that someone else was always lower on the social ladder. If African Americans had all the rights that whites had, that security would be gone. Violence, heckling and other expressions of hatred had often been used to intimidate blacks. But television now changed things. Even local events played out in a national forum, as the evening news was broadcast throughout the country. Ultimately, whites would have to stop acting on their prejudices.

A new fervor and belief in equality and freedom began to grow among black and white Americans in the 1960s—much as it had a century before during the formation of the abolition movement—and this civil rights movement would be led by a young southern African-American preacher, Martin Luther King, Jr. Following the nonviolent tactics of Indian leader Mohandas Gandhi, King led boycotts, sit-ins, freedom rides and mass marches to spread his views, change unfair laws and establish more just practices.

Leaders such as Stokely Carmichael and Malcolm X, meanwhile, preached more Afrocentric paths, promoting black power, self-sufficiency and self-imposed black separatism—ideals that enhanced a sense of ethnic pride.

But nearly 400 years after the first slave ship arrived on American shores, not enough progress has been made. Violence and frustration have haunted black ghettos, and leaders are caught between justified impatience and a society slow to move toward multiculturalism. The future of what some observers call the nation's multiracial, multicultural democratic experiment hangs in the balance and will only be assured when racism and economic denial are no longer seen, as Martin Luther King, Jr., once said, "as superficial blemishes," but are recognized as a disease potentially fatal to the entire democracy.

In this book we've been able to explore only a tiny sliver of this four-century legacy of the African-American experience, with its richness and complexity. From the period before the Civil War, we look at the early African-American church and its involvement in the abolitionist movement, free African-Americans in New England, Frederick Douglass and his fight for the abolition of slavery, Harriet Tubman and the Underground Railroad and plantation slavery and the career of Booker T. Washington. We look at the Exoduster (technically, pre-Exoduster) settlement of Nicodemus, Kansas; the Buffalo Soldiers in Arizona, New Mexico, Kansas and Montana; black entrepreneur Maggie Lena Walker; educator and activist Mary McLeod Bethune; and civil rights leader Martin Luther King, Jr.

For more places and sources to explore, we encourage you to look at the Exploring Further section at the end of each chapter and More Places to Visit and More Reading Sources at the end of this book.

The African Meeting House

THE OLDEST EXISTING AFRICAN-AMERICAN CHURCH
Boston, Massachusetts

AT A GLANCE

Built: 1806

Oldest African-American church building still in existence
A brick meetinghouse, originally built as the first black church in Boston.
It is also known as the birthplace of the abolitionist movement.

Address:

Boston African-American
National Historic Site
Abiel Smith School
46 Joy Street
Boston, MA 02114-4025
(617) 742-5415

African Meeting House on Joy Street in Boston, ca. 1895 (Society for the Preservation of New England Antiquities)

> *Originally established as the African Meeting House, this simple, brick building is known as the birthplace of the abolitionist movement. In the 19th century it served as a forum for leading exponents of the antislavery cause, including Frederick Douglass, William Nell, William Lloyd Garrison, Maria Stewart, Charles Summer and many others.*

We have met to-night in this obscure school-house;
our numbers are few and our influence limited; but, mark
my prediction. . . . We shall shake the Nation.

—William Lloyd Garrison, January 6, 1832, on exiting
a meeting at the African Meeting House

♦ ♦ ♦ ♦ ♦

The African Meeting House is an unassuming, quiet brick building located on Beacon Hill in what was once the heart of Boston's African-American community. From its unimposing exterior no one would ever guess this building's historic significance. But it was here that Frederick Douglass recruited black men to join the historic 54th Massachusetts Regiment during the Civil War, here that white abolitionist William Lloyd Garrison launched the New England Anti-Slavery Society, and here that the great issues affecting the African-American community were debated in the years preceding the Civil War.

Boston was founded in 1630, and the first Africans arrived eight years later, in February 1638. They were brought as slaves, purchased on Providence Isle, a Puritan colony off the coast of Central America. By 1705, the slave population in Boston numbered more than 400, and the beginnings of a free black community had also started to form in the town's North End section. Slavery was abolished in the Commonwealth of Massachusetts in 1738. It was the only state in the Union that reported no slave population when the first federal census was taken in 1790, after the Revolutionary War and the formation of the new nation. The Declaration of Independence had left ambiguity about the legality of slavery in the

United States, and the issue remained unresolved for the entire nation throughout the first 65 years of the 1800s. In the meantime, progress moved slowly. As a start, in 1784, the New England states Vermont, Massachusetts, New Hampshire, Connecticut and Rhode Island abolished the slave trade.

In 1796, 20 years after the American Revolution began, leaders of the black community in Boston formed the African Society. The society met at first in homes and helped organize the community, provide funds to those in need and help African Americans find work.

By the beginning of the 19th century, the African-American community in Boston numbered nearly 1,100, and by 1820 had increased to 1,690, nearly 4 percent of the city's total population. But freedom and numbers did not by any means translate to equal and just treatment, and in virtually every aspect of life, blacks faced discrimination and lack of power—in churches, schools, employment and social life.

Some African Americans had begun to think the best answer to their plight was to return to Africa. On that vast continent, they thought, they could found a colony where they could build their own legal system and government. In 1787 members of the first known black organization in America, the African Union Society in Rhode Island, had already corresponded with leaders of the black Bostonian community about this idea. Bostonian African Americans, though, along with the majority of blacks throughout the country, were against leaving the United States. They believed that they had already made American soil their home. Many had fought in the Revolutionary War, and almost all had hopes for the new constitutional government. They saw colonization as a solution to interracial problems promoted primarily by whites who didn't want to accommodate blacks, and Bostonian African Americans resolved to stay and fight for equality.

In that fight the foundation of the African Meeting House in 1806 represented the establishment of an important battleground for freedom, justice and equality. The African Society in Boston had found an open, farmland area on the north slope of Beacon Hill—an area known as the West End—where there was room to establish better living conditions than in the squalid North End. They encouraged members of the neighborhood to move there, thereby establishing a core neighborhood still located near the jobs downtown and the wealthy white families on Beacon Hill, where many blacks worked as servants. To draw African Americans to the area, leaders of the community decided to establish a meetinghouse.

But the meetinghouse was really more than just a place for people to gather. It also became a church building housing an all-black Baptist church, the First African Baptist Church, established the preceding year. In the 18th century black Baptists had attended white churches. But they were relegated to the galleries, where they could only hear, not see, the preacher. And they were allowed to participate only in church services and ceremonies, such as weddings and funerals. They had no power or part in the political life of the church. Tired of the discrimination, they decided to splinter off from the main Baptist church to found their own independent black church movement in Boston, and to construct a church building of their own, which became the African Meeting House.

In July 1805 Scipio Dalton and Cato Gardner, two black members of the First Baptist Church in Boston and members of the African Society, wrote to the First and Second Baptist Churches in Boston (both primarily white) to ask for their support in establishing a church for black citizens. Both churches sent their ministers and deacons.

The church was established August 8, 1805 with 20 members, and Thomas Paul—a young black Baptist preacher who had already been holding services in the West End schoolhouse—was made the pastor. But there was no building.

So members of the African Society began raising funds—Cato Gardner alone raised $1,500. Land was purchased in 1805 and building began soon afterward. With support pouring in from both the white and black community statewide, the $7,500 needed to finish the construction was raised, and the contruction was finished and dedicated in 1806. As reported in the inner pages of the December 8, 1806 edition of Boston's *Independent Chronicle,*

> On Thursday last, the African Meeting House, at West-Boston, was dedicated to the worship of God. At the same time the Rev. Thomas Paul, a man of colour, was introduced to the pastoral care of the African Baptist Church, in that place. . . . Though the weather was very unfavourable, the assembly was large and respectable.—The singing was excellent and appropriate.

Inside the African Meeting House—as it was in the 1930s. (Society for the Preservation of New England Antiquities)

The multipurpose red-brick building was designed to be used, not only for church services and meetings of the community, but also to house a schoolroom for black children. It was to be a place "for the education of the people of colour of all denominations," as stated by the *Chronicle*. It would prove to be a focal point for strength and cooperation in the black community. The schoolroom, inspired by the poor treatment that African-American children received in white schools, was intended to provide a better, more just educational environment for the community's children. And it was the precursor to the establishment of the Abiel Smith School next door (see A Close-Up). But in retrospect many black leaders came to think that establishing black churches and schools created a separatist environment that fostered segregationism.

William C. Nell, who was born in Boston in 1816 and attended school in the basement of the African Meeting House, came to be strongly outspoken on this subject. As a student he had successfully competed in a Boston-wide competition for the Franklin Medal, which was awarded annually by the Boston School Committee to students of outstanding scholastic achievement. But because of his race, Nell was not invited to the awards dinner. He was, however, allowed to serve at it. Stung by this degradation, Nell became a journalist, determined to fight this kind of discrimination wherever he saw it.

The idea of colonization in Africa continued to divide the black community, and Nell was strongly against it. Blacks both enslaved and free had given of themselves for two centuries to help establish the United States and had earned the right to stay. Nonetheless, in 1822, a group of African Americans did travel to the West Coast of Africa to found Liberia. But in 1829 the First African Baptist Church debated the issue and passed a resolution condemning the colonization.

The African Meeting House became a key focal point for the movement against slavery. Although Boston's African Americans were free, true freedom would never come to the black community until slavery was abolished throughout the nation. The African Meeting House welcomed debate and open discussion of opinions, and many speakers used its lectern to address the public of Boston.

One of the first American women to speak out publicly on political issues of any kind was a black abolitionist and activist for women's rights named

Maria Stewart, who spoke there in 1833. Her remarks were cogent and eloquent. ". . . it is not the color of the skin that makes the man or the woman," she told her audience, "but the principle formed in the soul. Brilliant wit will shine, come from whence it will; and genius and talent will not hide the brightness of its lustre."

White abolitionist William Lloyd Garrison could find no place in Boston to hold his antislavery rallies in 1832, but the African Meeting House welcomed him then and many times thereafter. In the Preamble to the Constitution of the New England Anti-Slavery Society read aloud at the African Meeting House on January 6, 1832, Garrison spoke out for freedom:

> We, the undersigned, hold that every person, of full age and sane mind, has a right to immediate freedom from personal bondage of whatsoever kind, unless imposed by the sentence of the law, for the commission of some crime. We hold that man cannot, consistently with reason, religion, and the eternal and immutable principles of justice, be the property of man. We hold that whoever retains his fellow-man in bondage is guilty of a grievous wrong. We hold that a mere difference of complexion is no reason why any man should be deprived of any of his natural rights, or subjected to any political disability. While we advance these opinions as the principles on which we intend to act, we declare that we will not operate on the existing relations of society by other than peaceful and lawful means, and that we will give no countenance to violence or insurrection.

As he left the African Meeting House that night, Garrison jubilantly exclaimed, ". . . mark my prediction. . . . We shall shake the Nation."

Later, in July of that same year, Garrison told another African Meeting House gathering, "The number [of abolitionists] is increasing with singular rapidity. The standard which has been lifted up in Boston is attracting the gaze of the nation, and inspiring the drooping hearts of thousands with hope and courage."

In this same hall in 1860, abolitionist and former slave Frederick Douglass spoke passionately in memory of John Brown, the leader of a raid on Harper's Ferry. Brown had attempted to spark a revolt of slaves and had become a martyr to the cause of abolition.

When the Civil War began in 1861, many black Bostonians wanted to help fight on the Union side, but President Lincoln did not allow African

Americans to join the Union military until 1863. At that time, the African Meeting House became the recruitment center for the black 54th Massachusetts Regiment, and African Americans came to enlist from all over, including fugitive slaves from Canada.

After the war Boston became an attractive city to former slaves moving north, and by the mid-1890s the church membership had expanded to 400 and had outgrown the African Meeting House. Many members of the African-American community had begun to move away from Beacon Hill, and the church—which by now was called the First Independent Baptist Church (no longer restricted to black membership)—decided to move to a larger church building at the corner of Camden and Tremont Streets in Roxbury, a district where many of the members had moved. In 1915 this congregation changed its name to the People's Baptist Church, which it remains today.

Today visitors of the reconstructed African Meeting House can imagine what it was like in the days when the building served as church, school and meetinghouse, the scene of impassioned antislavery speeches and much intense debate. Because restoration is slow and still in progress, visitors must imagine the simple wooden pews that once lined the floor of the sanctuary—now temporarily replaced by red chairs. But the simple altar and plain architecture speak of a time more focused on issues and principles than pomp and circumstance. The unadorned curved arches of the sanctuary's 1½-story windows, echoed by the arched entrance doorways at street level, are among the few decorative architectural details of this plain, utilitarian structure, which remains today as a veritable storehouse of African-American history.

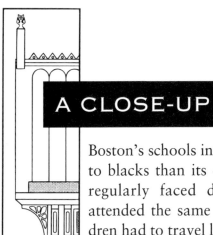

A CLOSE-UP ABIEL SMITH SCHOOL

Boston's schools in the 18th century were even less welcoming to blacks than its churches were. African-American children regularly faced discrimination there, even though they attended the same schools as did white children. Black children had to travel long distances to reach school—because the buildings were never located conveniently for them—and they usually were placed in vocational classes without regard for their aptitude. Sometimes they were not allowed to attend class, out of fear that they might carry some disease. Even minor infractions were dealt with more harshly when the offender was an African-American child. Although their parents made petitions and brought court suits for equal treatment, no progress was made. And the Boston School Committee refused to establish a separate, all-black school.

So home schooling began in the African-American community, with black parents organizing local schools in their homes as early as 1798. The schoolroom of the African Meeting House was completed in 1808, and for 26 years the school met in the basement.

In the early 1830s, however, a white philanthropist named Abiel Smith left an endowment to aid in the education of black children. In 1834, the Abiel Smith School was built next to the African Meeting House on the corner of Smith Court and Joy Street. It was a simple, boxlike structure, a two-story brick building with a basement—space enough for classes, serving as many as 78 or more students at one time. Once the Abiel Smith School opened, the schoolroom in the basement of the African Meeting House was used for adult classes and other purposes.

By 1840, however, under the leadership of William Nell—who had become a militant African-American spokesperson for integration and abolition of slavery—a group of blacks and whites petitioned the Boston School Committee for equal school rights for black students. They demanded desegregation of Boston's public schools, and Nell led a boycott for 11 years against the all-black Abiel Smith School. Of course, boycotters faced the problem that black children could not readily attend the white schools, either. So boycotting students during those years attended classes in the basement of the African Meeting House, once again.

The Equal Rights School Committee was founded by Nell in 1850. In 1855 legislation closed the blacks-only Abiel Smith School next to the African Meeting House. Black children entered the Boston public schools that fall, on an equal footing for the first time.

Today the Abiel Smith School looks much the way it did in 1834 from the outside. Inside, for the moment, it houses the administrative offices of the museum and a bookstore, but the museum's curator has placed renovation and restoration of the interior of this building high on the list of priorities. In the future visitors will be able to visit a place that evokes, both inside and out, an important segment of African-American history.

Abiel Smith Court ca. 1895: On the left, in the foreground, is Abiel Smith School. The African Meeting House is next door. (Society for the Preservation of New England Antiquities)

PRESERVING IT FOR THE FUTURE

From the time of its foundation in 1964, the Museum of Afro-American History in Boston recognized the African Meeting House as a historical site worthy of preservation. In 1972 the museum purchased the site from the Jewish congregation that had bought it in 1898 and had used it as a synagogue. Unfortunately, fire ravaged the building in 1973 during restoration, causing considerable damage, including destruction of the roof. The city threatened to demolish the structure, but funding for a temporary roof was found by members of the museum and the building was saved.

In 1974 the African Meeting House was designated a National Historic Landmark, and in 1980 Congress passed a bill establishing the African Meeting House and all the other sites on the Black Heritage Trail (see Exploring Further) as components of a new National Historic Site. The African Meeting House, however, remains the property of the museum, the only site on the Heritage Trail that is black owned.

EXPLORING ♦ FURTHER

Books on the Abolitionist Movement and the African Meeting House

Borman, Ernest, ed. *Forerunners of Black Power: The Rhetoric of Abolition.* Englewood Cliffs, New Jersey: Prentice-Hall, 1971.

Garrison, Wendell Phillips, and Francis Jackson Garrison, eds. *William Lloyd Garrison.* New York: Century, 1885.

Hayden, Robert C., and the staff of the Museum of Afro-American History. *The African Meeting House in Boston: A Celebration of History.* Boston: A Companion Press Book, The Museum of Afro-American History, 1987.

Katz, William Loren, *Breaking the Chains: African American Slave Resistance.* New York: Atheneum, 1990.

Related Places

Black Heritage Trail
Boston, Massachusetts

Information: Boston African American National Historic Site, Abiel Smith School, 46 Joy Street, Boston, MA 02114-4025, (617) 742-5415

Developed under the guidance of the Boston African American National Historic Site, the Black Heritage Trail is a walking tour including 14 sites representative of African American life in Boston between 1800 and 1900. One of these is the African Meeting House. Others are: Robert Gould Shaw 54th Massachusetts Regiment Memorial, George Middleton House,

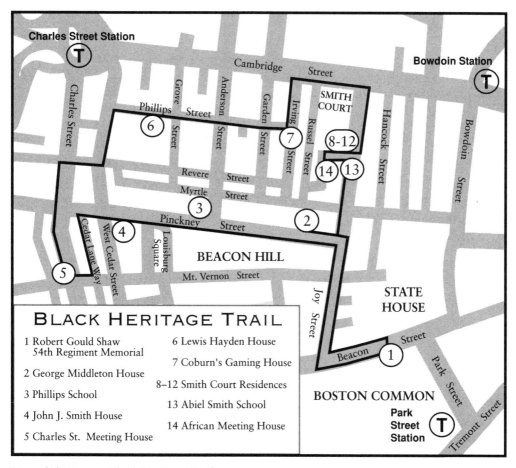

Map of the Boston Black Heritage Trail

Phillips School (one of Boston's first schools to have an integrated student body), John J. Smith House, Charles Street Meeting House, Lewis Hayden House, Coburn's Gaming House, the Smith Court Residences, and Abiel Smith School. Of the buildings on this trail, however, only the African Meeting House and the Abiel Smith School are open to the public.

The African Meeting House on Nantucket
Pleasant Street and York (Five Corners)
P.O. Box 1802
Nantucket, MA 02554
(508) 228-4058

Opening to the public in 1998, this small restored structure is the only historical building remaining on Nantucket Island that was central to the African-American community, which dates back as far as the 1700s. Slavery was abolished on Nantucket in 1770. Thereafter some 300 free African Americans formed a vital part of the community as tradespeople, barbers, clergy and one—Absalom Boston—as master of his own sailing vessel, which had an all-black crew. Boston was among the original builders of the Nantucket edifice, which served as a church, a school for African-American children and a meetinghouse. The Friends of the African Meeting House on Nantucket have also put together a Nantucket Black Heritage Trail, guided by a brochure available from them or from the Museum of Afro-American History, 46 Joy Street, Boston, MA 02114.

The Old Stone House

ACADEMY BUILT BY ALEXANDER LUCIUS TWILIGHT, EDUCATOR
Brownington, Vermont

AT A GLANCE

Built: 1834–36
Academy (1836–59) built by Alexander Lucius Twilight
and directed by him, 1836–57
A four-story, granite building built as a dormitory and as classroom space
for Brownington Academy, as the Orleans County Grammar School was
locally known. He called the new structure Athenian Hall, but as time
passed everyone just called it the Old Stone House.

Mailing Address:
Old Stone House Museum
c/o the Orleans County Historical Society
Rural Route 1, Box 500
Orleans, VT 05860

Visiting Address:
Old Stone House Museum
Brownington, Vermont 05860
(802) 754-2022

The first black to graduate from an American college, Alexander Lucius Twilight believed fervently in the cause of education. In 1829, Twilight came to Brownington, Vermont, and seeing the need for a better school, built a four-story structure of granite, using his own resources.

When unshakable Principal meets adverse Circumstance, bet on the Principal—if he's a barrel-chested, rock-ribbed, hard-nosed Vermonter with a vision.

—Gregor Hileman, Editor,
Middlebury College News Letter

◆ ◆ ◆ ◆ ◆

Located in remote northeastern Vermont, a towering stone building keeps watch over the sleepy little town of Brownington and the granite-laden hills of Orleans County. For a century and a half, this massive structure, now known as the Old Stone House, has dominated the landscape. The Reverend Alexander Lucius Twilight (1795–1857), who taught school and preached in Brownington, began the building in 1834, completing it in 1836. Today, restored to its original appearance, it stands as a monument to the man who built it, the first black American college graduate and a man of considerable determination and will.

Born September 23, 1795 in Bradford, Vermont, Alexander Lucius Twilight was the third of six children of Ichabod and Mary Twilight, free African Americans who had come to Vermont from Plattsburgh, New York. Ichabod died when Alexander was only eight. To pay for his room and board, Alexander was indentured (bound by mutual agreement to serve until a debt is paid) to a neighboring farmer. He must have been both industrious and frugal, however, earning enough extra to buy himself free of his indenture service a year early, in 1815. He enrolled in the nearby Orange County Grammar School in Randolph, Vermont, and within six years he had completed the secondary-school curriculum and two years of college coursework. In 1821 he entered Middlebury College in western Vermont, receiving an A.B. degree from Middlebury in 1823.

Alexander married Mercy Ladd Merrill, the sister of a Middlebury classmate, in 1826. He studied theology during this time, receiving a license to preach in 1827. After teaching briefly elsewhere, he accepted a teaching position in 1829 at the Orleans County Grammar School, of which he later became principal. He also served as minister of the local church from 1829 to 1834, holding services on the second floor of the school building. (Later, in 1841, a church would be built next door, which visitors can still visit today.) When they arrived in Brownington, the Twilights moved into a tiny three-room frame homestead near the school—a house so small that Twilight immediately began building a larger house next to it.

At that time, Brownington was a growing community, the center of Orleans County's political, social and educational life. The main road running through town was part of Hinman Road, a major arterial for the county as far back as the early 1790s. The stage route to Montreal, Canada, ran along Hinman Rod from Boston, and while it's now remote and off the beaten path, in 1829, Brownington was vigorous and thriving.

Twilight was a stern but charismatic teacher, and the school enrollment rose during his tenure. "He seldom failed to get the good will and high esteem of his pupils," a former student wrote years later. "His power to influence, stimulate, and direct them in regard to their character, studies, and future pursuits was great."

The Orleans County Grammar School attracted students from all over the county, and those whose families didn't live in Brownington needed a place to stay during the school term. Twilight built his own house large enough to accommodate several students—three boys and two girls boarded with the Twilights in 1830. But by 1834 he could see that a larger facility with dormitory space would enable the school to serve many more students. And so he set about with his plans for Athenian Hall, the famous structure that today is known as the Old Stone House. But the school board never supported Twilight's plans, and while they didn't prevent him from carrying them out, they also made no funds available for its completion. Not easily stopped once his mind was made up, however, Twilight undertook the job himself.

The Old Stone House, Brownington Village Historic District (Courtesy of the Orleans County Historical Society)

While no correspondence, plans or any other documents remain pertaining specifically to the construction and how it was carried out, what is certain is that Twilight spearheaded the planning and execution, completely without funding from the county or support from the school board.

Teachers were no more well paid in those days than they are now, comparatively speaking, and with little written documentation about how Twilight could have built such a building with only a teacher's resources, a legend has sprung up to explain how it was done. When Twilight resolved to build the Old Stone House, the story goes, he quarried the stones himself from neighboring fields and enlisted the help of a single ox to cart the stones to the site and lift them into place. Using a wooden or earthen staging, or scaffolding, he placed the ox on a treadmill located on the staging. The power of the treadmill enabled him to lift the stones into place. As the walls rose, he increased the level of the staging. Then, once the structure was complete, since he had no way to lower the ox to the ground, Twilight slaughtered the ox for the celebration feast. How much of this story is true is open to question, but a massive ox yoke and iron pry allegedly used in the construction remain on display today at the Old Stone House Museum.

It's a wonderful legend, but the facts may have been more mundane. The ox probably did not remain in place throughout the building process, and it probably didn't get served up for dinner. A few, perhaps more plausible, explanations for how Twilight managed the enormous task have also been proposed. Cyrus Eaton, who had recently built on adjacent land, may have loaned him some funds. Or Twilight may have obtained some funds from his wife or his wife's family. Regardless, the edifice is a monument to the solid determination of one man.

The finished building is big, with 65 windows and, on the first floor, a kitchen, dining room, music parlor, 14 student rooms and 6 recitation rooms. Two classrooms and an assembly hall made up the fourth-floor facilities. While it had no central heat, the building had one large fireplace and numerous brazier alcoves, or mini-fireplaces, in the public rooms of the first two floors. To heat the rooms, hot coals were carried daily in pots from the central fireplace to the braziers, each of which was vented by a separate small chimney. The large fireplace, which visitors can still view, was the central hub of life at the school. Here Mercy Twilight cooked most of the meals and baked bread for the entire school in ovens heated by the main hearth's flames. Big iron stoves warmed the hall on the third floor and the two large classrooms on the top floor.

Inside, the walls are plastered, but the woodwork above the first floor remains unpainted and unfinished today as it did in the days when students lived and studied there. There was, of course, no indoor plumb-

Alexander L. Twilight (1795– 1857)   (Courtesy of the Orleans County Historical Society)

ing. A cistern outside collected rainwater that was funneled inside to the kitchen via a system of pipes, and an adjacent barn housed the outhouses, although neither barn nor outhouses remain.

With the great stone structure only just completed, in 1836 Twilight was elected to the Vermont legislature, becoming one of the first black state representatives. He served as legislator in Montpelier, the state capital, during the 1836–37 session, where he argued passionately for his foremost cause: the establishment of a strong educational system. The residents of the nearby town of Craftsbury had proposed that the land rents in their area supporting the Brownington school should be funneled into a school system of their own. Twilight contended that the precedent was a bad one. He maintained that centralized schools, along the lines of his own academy, with well-educated instructors and good facilities, were far preferable to a hodgepodge mixture of small, community-supported schools of uneven quality. History shows that Twilight's argument was sound. He may have won the battle at that time, but eventually the centralized school lost out. Within 20 years the countryside of Vermont was dotted with little one-room schools, usually taught by amateur teachers, because schools for teacher education were rare. However, in Twilight's centralized, all-county school, the headmaster could provide direction, and experienced fellow teachers could offer example and suggestions—advantages the novice teacher would never gain in small local schools.

By the time that Twilight came back from his session in Montpelier, he was ready to provide that kind of guidance in the Athenian Hall. By now alive with the enthusiastic voices of children away from home for the first time, the hall provided a home away from home. Students came for a four-term school year, with 12 weeks per term, to study a broad curriculum that included "common English" (tuition $2.00 per term); Latin, Greek, Italian, Spanish, or "higher English" (at $3.00); written or spoken French ($3.50) and vocal music ($.50). Lectures in the sciences were also available, including natural philosophy, chemistry, geology, astronomy, botany and agriculture. Twilight lectured on the Bible on Sunday evenings. Students followed an intense regime, studying from 9:00 A.M. to 7:00 P.M. and attending required church on Sundays. Visitors can still see the simply designed student row-desks, of which four still remain—the seat of one desk attached to one behind, the top of each desk formed by a plain 2-inch plank.

During his 21 years of teaching, Twilight helped to shape the lives of some 3,000 students, many of whom later became mayors, teachers, businesspeople and missionaries, scattered all over the nation. Brownington Academy's list of alumni includes an impressive number of well-known names, such as: William B. Strong, who became president of the Atchison, Topeka & Santa Fe Railroad; his brother, Henry Strong, mayor of Beloit, Wisconsin; Portius Baxter, who served as a member of the U.S. Congress from Vermont during the Civil War; and Tyler Stewart, a U.S. consul to Spain.

Twilight temporarily retired from both preaching and teaching in Brownington in 1847, although he continued to teach in nearby schools in Quebec. In 1852, however, he was called back to Brownington and appointed headmaster of Brownington Academy, also returning to the pulpit.

Twilight continued as headmaster and minister until he suffered a stroke in 1855 that left him paralyzed, forcing his retirement. He died in 1857 at the age of 62. The nearby cemetery of the church in which Twilight preached contains the burial sites and gravestones of Alexander and Mercy Twilight. The two graves, located at the front of the cemetery, look out toward the Old Stone House that Twilight built, a monument to his indomitable spirit and will.

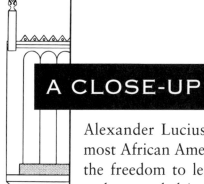

BLACK SCHOLARS IN NEW ENGLAND, 1820S

Alexander Lucius Twilight was unusual. At a time when most African Americans lived in slavery, without so much as the freedom to learn the alphabet, Twilight was born free and succeeded in gaining a college education. As a boy he was indentured, but he was able to shorten his committed time of service by purchasing his final year. He enrolled in school and pursued a college education, graduating from Middlebury College in Vermont in 1823. He was the first but not the only African American to do so. In 1826 Edward A. Jones—son of a hotel keeper in Charleston, South Carolina—graduated on August 23 from Amherst College in Massachusetts, while John Russwurm received a bachelor's degree two weeks later from Bowdoin College in Maine.

Russwurm, a Jamaican who had prepared for college in New York City, delivered the oration for his graduating class and was the first black to join a college fraternity. Russwurm went on to become cofounder and copublisher of the first U.S. black-owned and -edited newspaper, *Freedom's Journal*, which eventually had distribution in 11 states. A strong supporter of creating a colony in Africa composed of African Americans, Russwurm left for Liberia in 1829 and served there as governor of Maryland Colony from 1836 until his death in 1851.

Only a few more blacks graduated from New England colleges prior to the Civil War, however. Oberlin College—the country's first coeducational college, founded in 1833 in Ohio—did more than any other college in the country for educating blacks prior to 1865. The first African-American woman to obtain a bachelor of arts degree received it from Oberlin in 1862. In fact, it was one of Oberlin's specific missions to educate abolitionists. By the Civil War about one-third of the student body was black, while black slaves in the South continued to be forbidden even the most rudimentary education. The right to an education would become one of the keys to a brighter future for many African Americans after the Civil War.

PRESERVING IT FOR THE FUTURE

Two years after Twilight's death in 1857, the school that he had established closed down. A few years later his wife sold the Old Stone House to a local family in Orleans County. For many years the house was used as a private residence and boardinghouse, until 1918, when the Orleans County Historical Society purchased the building for $500. Since that time, the Historical Society has worked to restore and preserve the structure, replacing the roof in 1983 and seven chimney tops that had been cut off during previous reroofing. Today historical exhibits from all over Orleans County can be seen in the 25 rooms of Alexander Twilight's Old Stone House.

The Twilight homestead building was given to the Historical Society in 1978 by the Perry family, owners of the Twilight farmhouse. The homestead structure, the Twilights' first home in Brownington, was built prior to 1829 on the land across the street from the Old Stone House. Later the Twilight farmhouse that now stands there was built adjacent to it, forming an L shape. When the Historical Society gained ownership of the homestead building, it was moved to its present site west of the Old Stone House. Renovations on the structure are still in progress, and when complete, the homestead building will house the society's collection of early farm tools and machinery.

EXPLORING ◆ FURTHER

Readings on Alexander Twilight

Hileman, Gregor. "The Iron-Willed Black Schoolmaster and His Granite Academy," *Middlebury College News Letter*, Spring 1974.
Nicolosi, Vincent. "Twilight Mystery," *Yankee*, June 1986.

Related Places

Brownington Village Historic District
Brownington, Vermont 05860
(802) 754-2022

Visitors to the Old Stone House can also take a walking tour of the surrounding village where Twilight lived, taught and preached. Across the road is the Twilight home (not open to the public), and nearby are the original Twilight homestead home (which has been moved to a location near the Old Stone House), the church where Twilight preached and the cemetery where Alexander and Mercy are buried. The home of Cyrus Eaton, built in 1834 and owned by the Historical Society, is also nearby. Eaton may have helped Twilight build the Old Stone House, was a trustee of the academy and sent two sons and a daughter to study there. Visitors can also view the site at the bottom of Prospect Hill where the Orange County Grammar School was located when Twilight first taught there, and they can climb the hill to the observatory, reconstructed to resemble the one used by Twilight's students. Across the village is the original schoolhouse of the Orange County Grammar School, now used as a grange hall.

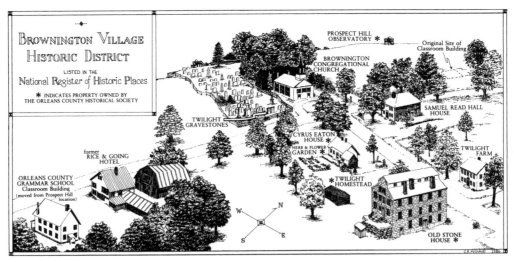

Map of the Brownington Village Historic District (C. R. Michaud, 1986. Courtesy of the Orleans County Historical Society)

Cedar Hill

HOME OF FREDERICK DOUGLASS, FREEDOM FIGHTER
Washington, D.C.

AT A GLANCE

Built: 1855–59

Home of Frederick Douglass, 1877–95

A 14-room brick house located on $15\frac{1}{2}$ acres in the Anacostia area of Washington, D.C., east of the Potomac River. The house has a broad front porch with a pediment overhead and columns in the southern style.

Address:

Cedar Hill
Frederick Douglass National Historic Site
1411 W Street, SE
Washington, DC 20016
(202) 426-5960

Cedar Hill, home of Frederick Douglass   (William Clark. Courtesy of the National Park Service)

> *Frank and to the point, Frederick Douglass left white listeners little room in their consciences for comfort to which he believed they had no right, as he fought to gain freedom for those still enslaved in this country before the Civil War.*

Fellow Citizens: Pardon me, and allow me to ask, why am I called to speak here today? What have I or those I represent to do with your national independence? Are the great principles of political freedom and natural justice, embodied in that Declaration of Independence, extended to us? And am I, therefore, called upon to bring our humble offering to the national altar, and to confess the benefits, and express devout gratitude for the blessings resulting from your independence to us? Would to God, both for your sakes and ours, that an affirmative answer could be truthfully returned to these questions.

—Frederick Douglass, in his Fourth of July 1853 speech

♦ ♦ ♦ ♦ ♦

In 1877 Frederick Douglass (1818–95) bought a large house on a 9³/₄-acre estate in the Anacostia district of Washington, D.C. When he purchased this lot, Douglass broke a "whites-only" covenant explicit in the deed, which prohibited the sale, rental or lease of the property to any "Negro, Mulatto, or anyone of African or Irish descent." The following year he purchased another 5³/₄ adjoining acres to the south. Douglass was not enchanted by the place's name, Van Hook's Hill, after former owner and land speculator John Van Hook. He was, however, delighted by its many towering cedar trees, as well as oaks, ashes, black walnuts and chestnuts; Douglas renamed the place Cedar Hill. In 1886 a reporter for the *Cincinnati Inquirer* described the estate as "a moderate-sized mansion on an elevation, surrounded by full grown trees, cedar, and firs and forest trees. This gives delightful shade and protection from the winds. The House is about 50 to 70 feet above the road, and high flights of steps lead up to it. . . ."

Here the venerable freedom fighter would spend the last 18 years of his life. For visitors to the National Historic Site, this beautiful home symbolizes, not only Douglass's accomplishments for African Americans and every American in the cause of freedom, but also the great personal stature he had achieved by the 60th year of his life.

Frederick Augustus Washington Bailey (as he was called at birth) was born a slave in February 1817, on a Maryland plantation, the son of Harriet Bailey, who was a slave. He never knew who his father was, although some historians have speculated he may have been his mother's master, Aaron Anthony. Separated from his mother shortly after birth, Douglass endured from childhood all the brutality and degradation of slavery. As a terror-stricken seven year old, he witnessed his Aunt Hester being harshly beaten with a heavy, yard-long whip. He later wrote:

Frederick Douglass   (Courtesy of the National Park Service)

I never shall forget it whilst I remember any thing. It was the first of a long series of such outrages, of which I was doomed to be a witness and a participant. It struck me with awful force. It was the blood-stained gate, the entrance to the hell of slavery through which I was about to pass.

Shortly after that he was sent to Baltimore, where he worked as a household servant for a man who had books in his home. During this time young Frederick decided that knowledge could be the pathway to freedom, and he taught himself to read and write. After serving under a number of owners, he broke for freedom for the first time in 1836, near St. Michael's, Maryland, but was recaptured.

Still a slave, Frederick met Anna Murray in Maryland that same year. She was a free woman, the daughter of former slaves. Two years after they first met, while Frederick was working as a ship's caulker in Baltimore, Anna succeeded in smuggling him more than half the money that he needed to buy a train ticket from Baltimore to Philadelphia. That train ride was his ride to freedom. To come up with the money, Anna sold her feather bed and also gave him the savings she had stored up during the nine years she had worked as a paid domestic servant. Two weeks after his escape in 1838, Frederick and Anna had arranged to meet in New York City, where they married, beginning a strong relationship that lasted 44 years. In 1839 their first child, Rosetta, was born and in late 1840 a son, Lewis. They were poor but free.

And once free, Frederick Augustus Washington Bailey changed his name to Frederick Douglass as an alias—one by which he has been known ever since. He and Anna moved to New Bedford, Massachusetts, where an escaped slave was safer from slave catchers and where he found work as a laborer. There he also met the white abolitionist and journalist William Lloyd Garrison and began to read Garrison's paper *The Liberator*. He became involved in some of the abolitionist meetings, and by 1841, while attending a convention of the Massachusetts Anti-Slavery Society in Nantucket, to his amazement, he was called on to speak. Douglass had spoken before to black audiences, but this audience was white and he was nervous. Nonetheless, as one reporter wrote, "Flinty hearts were pierced and cold ones melted by his eloquence." Douglass's career as an abolitionist orator had begun. He was asked to join the society as a lecturer.

By this time the abolitionist movement was gaining strength. More than 2,000 societies existed with memberships numbering over 200,000.

However, lectures did not often go smoothly—hecklers were nearly always present with sharp retorts, rotten eggs and overripe fruit. At one meeting, the going got very rough and Douglass came out badly bruised, his wrist broken, yet counted himself lucky.

Douglass soon became recognized as the most articulate spokesperson of the antislavery cause, an eloquent and persuasive voice in the fight for freedom. In 1845 he published his first autobiography, *Narrative of the Life of Frederick Douglass*. In 1847 he founded a newspaper, *The North Star*, which became a powerful organ in the fight against slavery and for equality, supporting industrial education for African Americans as well as women's right to vote.

When the *Dred Scott* decision was handed down by the U.S. Supreme Court, Douglass, like other abolitionists, was outraged. Scott was a slave who had lived for several years in free states, taken there by his master, and then returned to Missouri, a state in which slavery was legal. He then attempted to sue his master for his freedom. In 1857, the Supreme Court ruled that Scott had never ceased to be a slave, that slaves were not U.S. citizens and therefore could not take a case to court. Chief Justice Roger Taney spoke for the majority of justices with the pronouncement: "Negroes have no rights which the white man is bound to respect." To this Douglass replied, "The Supreme Court is not the only power in the world . . . Taney cannot bail out the ocean . . . or pluck the star of liberty from the Northern Sky."

Douglass was militant, he was articulate and he pulled no punches. "Yes," he would tell his listeners, "my blood has sprung out as the lash embedded itself in my flesh. And yet my master has the reputation of being a pious man and a good Christian. He was a class leader in the Methodist church. I have seen this pious class leader cross and tie the hands of one of his young female slaves, and lash her on the bare skin and justify the deed by the quotation from the Bible, 'he who knoweth his master's will and doeth it not, shall be beaten with many stripes.' "

Many listeners became abolitionists after hearing Douglass speak, and newspaper reporters noticed how he captivated audiences. One Detroit reporter wrote he was "the greatest orator of modern times." Douglass's voice was low, his language direct and eloquent, his manner compelling. He was 6 feet tall with "eyes dark with fire," as one listener remarked.

Douglass's concern for equality didn't stop with black men. He championed equal rights for all and played a key role in the women's rights convention held in Seneca Falls in 1848.

Unlike some other abolitionists, particularly Garrison, Douglass believed in working from within the political system, rather than relying strictly on moral persuasion, and a break came between the two men in 1851. But by 1861, after the outbreak of the Civil War, Douglass began to believe President Lincoln might not act to abolish slavery, and losing heart, he began to consider forming a colony of African Americans in Haiti. When Lincoln finally agreed, however, to allow blacks to fight in the military, Douglass helped recruit several black regiments for the Union army at the African Meeting House in Boston.

Abraham Lincoln was the first of four presidents advised by Douglass. They had political differences, but Douglass came to trust and admire Lincoln. "In his presence," Douglass wrote, "I am never reminded of my humble origins or of my unpopular color."

After the war, though hopeful that change would come about through working with the Republican Party, Douglass continued to speak out against the growing patterns of segregation, disfranchisement and mob violence against blacks. In the year before his death he gave a final, resounding speech against lynching. He always worked for the ultimate goal of assimilation of blacks into American society. Shortly before his death he put it this way:

> The real question is whether American justice, American liberty, American civilization, American law and American Christianity can be made to include and protect alike and forever all American citizens . . . whether this great nation shall conquer its prejudices, rise to the dignity of its professions, and proceed in the sublime course of truth and liberty . . . marked out for it.

At the age of 59, Frederick Douglass received an appointment as federal marshal of the District of Columbia. That same year, 1877, he and Anna moved to their new home, Cedar Hill. The place was their delight. From the front porch they had a stunning view of the capital city. On the wide, expansive grounds Douglass loved to walk and play croquet with his grandchildren. Douglass spent two years from 1879 to 1881 remodeling Cedar Hill—adding a wing at the back to house a kitchen, pantry and laundry. Many guests came to stay at the Douglass household, so at the same time he added bedrooms to the second floor. On the grounds, he planted a fruit orchard, a vegetable garden and a grape arbor, and he also added a carriage house, stable and other outbuildings.

Completing his term as federal marshal in 1881, he received another federal appointment as recorder of deeds for the District of Columbia. And the third version of his autobiography, *The Life and Times of Frederick Douglass*, was published the same year.

A visit to Douglass's home is like a step into a moment of his life—the place is full of memorabilia, personal possessions and gifts given to him by people such as antislavery writer Harriet Beecher Stowe and President Abraham Lincoln.

Entering the front door, it's easy to imagine Douglass's butler taking one's hat and coat to hang on the hooks nearby and accepting calling cards on a silver tray to take to Douglass, who no doubt would be working in his library. In the east parlor, the room reserved for entertaining, portraits of Anna and Frederick Douglass grace the walls, along with the likenesses of prominent friends. Here Douglass would relax and talk with his guests while he sat in the leather rocker given him in 1890 by the people of Haiti— where he served the United States as minister resident and consul general from 1889 to 1891. Often he would challenge friends to a game of checkers or listen with them to the music box.

The west parlor is less formal, more like a family room. Here the grandchildren romped, and against one wall stands the piano that Douglass's second wife, Helen, and Douglass's daughter, Rosetta, loved to play. Also in this room is a violin Douglass purchased for his grandson Joseph, who became one of the first black violin soloists to perform in Europe. Evidence of Douglass's interest in literature abound in this room as they do in his library. A portrait of Alexandre Dumas, who wrote two of Douglass's favorite books, *The Three Musketeers* and the *Count of Monte Cristo*, hangs on the wall, and on the mantel is a tile showing abolitionist-poet John Greenleaf Whittier's birthplace. Douglass counted other literary figures among his acquaintances, including the black poet Paul Laurence Dunbar, novelist Mark Twain, and essayist Ralph Waldo Emerson.

The dining room is the largest room at Cedar Hill, because the Douglass family loved to entertain. Around the large table many animated conversations took place among family and friends. In dramatic contrast to Douglass's childhood, when he ate cornmeal mush from a trough with a wooden spoon, in this room bountiful food served up in sparkling china on a table appointed in crisp white linen spoke eloquently of the prosperous life the Douglasses led. Douglass was a lively host and loved his role as family patriarch, and Anna Douglass loved to gather the entire family together in this room for Sunday dinners. The menu ranged from pork, lamb chops and oysters to cheese, bacon, roast beef and fish. Douglass didn't drink strong liquor, so Anna served cocoa, coffee and tea.

Upstairs visitors find Anna's bedroom especially touching. Described by a visitor at Cedar Hill as "dark, stout, and plain," Anna was the woman Douglass described as "the anchor of my life." She suffered from arthritis and rheumatism in her later years, and the invalid's chair that was used to move her to sun in the window is still by her bed. She lived only about four years at Cedar Hill before she died in 1882. In a biography, *My Mother as I Recall Her*, Anna's daughter Rosetta wrote, "During her wedded life of forty-four years, she was the same faithful ally, guarding as best she could every interest connected with my father, his lifework and the home."

In 1884, 18 months after Anna's death, Douglass remarried. Helen Pitts Douglass was 46 when she married Douglass, who was 66. An excellent administrator, she had worked for Douglass when he was recorder of deeds in Washington, D.C. Helen was a white woman who grew up the daughter of wealthy abolitionists in Upstate New York. She could trace her ancestry to the pilgrims who arrived on the *Mayflower*. Their wedding created a considerable stir, but Douglass replied to critics—among whom numbered some of his closest friends and family members—"My first wife was the color of my mother and the second the color of my father." Helen was equally calm. "Love came to me," she said, "and I was not afraid to marry the man I loved because of his color."

Helen and Douglass traveled together to England, France, Italy, Egypt and Greece in 1886–87 and were together 11 years, until he died. After his death she worked to transform Cedar Hill into a memorial to his life and work.

Frederick Douglass spent February 20, 1895 at a meeting of the National Council of Women in Washington. As always he showed his support for women's rights. That evening while recounting the day's events to Helen at Cedar Hill, he died of a massive stroke.

Helen Pitts Douglass (r), with Frederick Douglass   (Courtesy of the National Park Service)

But the ideal of freedom he fought for lives on. He envisioned a nation where character, not color or sex, would determine status; a nation based on honest principles of equal rights, dignity and justice.

A CLOSE-UP   THE LIBRARY

The library was the heartbeat of Frederick Douglass's day. Each morning he would get up early, take a walk around the grounds, come back for breakfast and then typically come to his favorite spot, the library, to spend five hours a day reading and writing at the roll-top desk near the windows. There he wrote many of his last speeches and his third and final autobiography, *The Life and Times of Frederick Douglass*. He sometimes used the small handpress that still stands near the fireplace to reproduce his speeches and pamphlets.

Douglass's desk at Cedar Hill   (Courtesy of the National Park Service)

The room has a comfortable feeling about it, from the carved-oak desk chair, which was made for the U.S. House of Representatives in 1857 and acquired by Douglass in 1859, to the patterned wallpaper and warm carpet. And from the homey arrangement of portraits and photographs over the fireplace and desk to the group of walking sticks standing by the window, ready for the next outing.

In this room Douglass kept his collection of some 1,200 books, on subjects ranging from politics, history, government and law to philosophy and theology. From the time he first taught himself to read and write, he always had a great thirst for knowledge, learning to speak and read several languages and reading avidly. Through education, he believed, one gains self-respect and self-determination in the face of the many obstacles and setbacks one might encounter.

In this room visitors can sense both the intellectual curiosity and the self-confidence of this man who fought for freedom so passionately. And they can sense his love of people and the arts. Photographs of people whom he knew and loved surround his desk, people of influence who had joined him in his struggle for human rights: Susan B. Anthony, William Lloyd Garrison, John Brown, Gerrit Smith and Henry Garnet (who was, like Douglass, a former slave). In one corner sit his violin case and music stand—a self-taught musician, he loved to play Scottish reels on his violin and often entertained friends and family in the west parlor.

This is the sort of room that every writer or thinker would love, with its philosophers' busts, pens and ledger books ready for writing, the sun pouring through the curtains, and Douglass well deserved it, for in his words:

> To those who have suffered in slavery I can say, I, too, have suffered. . . .
> To those who have battled for liberty, brotherhood, and citizenship I
> can say, I, too, have battled.

PRESERVING IT FOR THE FUTURE

After Douglass's death in 1895, his second wife, Helen Pitts Douglass, worked to preserve Cedar Hill as a memorial. She founded the Frederick

Douglass Memorial and Historical Association in 1900, which in 1916 joined with the National Association of Colored Women's Clubs. Maintenance and preservation of the house was coordinated by these two groups for nearly 50 years, until 1962, when they gave it to the people of the United States. On September 5, 1962 President John F. Kennedy signed a bill assigning responsibility for the site to the National Park Service. Since that time the Park Service restored the house over a 10-year period to its original appearance. In 1972 the Frederick Douglass Home opened to the public.

EXPLORING ◆ FURTHER

Books by Frederick Douglass

Douglass, Frederick. *Narrative of the Life of Frederick Douglass, An American Slave, Written by Himself.* 1845. Reprint, New York: St. Martin's Press, 1993.

———. *My Bondage and My Freedom.* 1855. Reprint, New York: Dover, 1969.

———. *The Life and Times of Frederick Douglass, Written by Himself.* 1881. Reprint, New York: St. Martin's Press, 1994.

———. *The Mind and Heart of Frederick Douglass.* Edited by Barbara Ritchie. New York: Crowell, 1968.

Douglass Books on the Internet

Project Gutenberg provides the full text on-line of the following Douglass works:

Narrative of the Life of Frederick Douglass, an American Slave and *Collected Articles of Frederick Douglass, a Slave.* Search on: Project Gutenberg.

Readings about Frederick Douglass

Banta, Melissa. *Frederick Douglass: Voice of Liberty.* New York: Chelsea House, 1993.

Bontemps, Arna. *Free at Last: The Life of Frederick Douglass.* New York: Dodd Mead, 1971.

Cooper, Mark A. Sr., ed. *Dear Father . . . Letters to Frederick Douglass from His Children, 1850–1894.* Philadelphia: Fulmore Press, 1990.

Huggins, Nathan J. *Slave and Citizen: The Life of Frederick Douglass.* Boston: Little, Brown, 1980.

McFeely, William S. *Frederick Douglass.* New York: W.W. Norton, 1991.

McKissack, Pat. *Frederick Douglass: The Black Lion.* Chicago: Children's Press, 1987.

Miller, Douglas T. *Frederick Douglass and the Fight for Freedom.* Makers of America series, edited by John Anthony Scott. New York: Facts On File, 1988.

Preston, Dickson J. *Young Frederick Douglass: The Maryland Years.* Baltimore: Johns Hopkins University Press, 1980.

Multimedia Software

The Douglass Project, A Multimedia Presentation for Windows

Reid-C Software
P.O. Box 512
Camp Springs, MD 20757
(301) 449-6474

Demonstration disk can be downloaded free from Compuserve or from the REID-C bulletin board at (301) 449-0419. Provides a visual tour of the house and grounds at Cedar Hill, text of selected writings by Douglass and brief biographical information about Douglass.

Harriet Tubman House

HOME OF AN UNDERGROUND RAILROAD CONDUCTOR
Auburn, New York

AT A GLANCE

Built: ca. 1850

Underground Railroad Conductor Harriet Tubman's home 1857–1913.
Home for aged and indigent blacks, established
by Harriet Tubman, 1908–1914.

Modest two-story frame house, purchased by
Harriet Tubman from Auburn, New York abolitionist
and politician William H. Seward.

Address:

Harriet Tubman House
180 South Street
Auburn, NY 13021
(315) 252-2081

According to baritone singer Paul Robeson, Harriet Tubman was the leader
that black singers really had in mind in the mid-1800s when they sang the
spiritual "Go Down, Moses"—a plea to the leader of the children of Israel to go
down to Egypt and lead his people out of bondage and into the Promised
Land. Tubman, a former slave, made 19 trips into the South, at great
personal risk, to lead some 300 people out of slavery in the 1850s.

... probably the most remarkable woman of this age ... she
has performed more wonderful deeds by the native power of
her own spirit than any other. ... [and] with her simple brave
motto, "I can't die but once," she began the work which has
made her Moses, the deliverer of her people.

—*Commonwealth*, July 17, 1863.

♦ ♦ ♦ ♦ ♦

N othing extraordinary strikes the eye about the medium-sized house
at 180 South Street in the small town of Auburn, in the Finger Lakes
region of Upstate New York. It's a simple two-story frame house
with a wide veranda running along the front and both sides. The surrounding land is heavily wooded and thick with underbrush. Fruit trees surround
the house. Inside on the ground floor there is a parlor, dining room, kitchen,
and a small bedroom. Upstairs five more rooms and a bathroom offer additional space for guests. The sparse furnishings date back to the early 1900s,
and there is a curious quiet to the place. Only when the tour guide begins to
talk does the history of the house really emerge. A tunnel in the basement
used to offer an emergency hiding place to fugitive slaves, she explains, and
from behind false closet doors upstairs, secret passageways lead out of the
house to the fields. Just a precaution, she admits, probably not ever used. But
the former owner of this quiet, outwardly commonplace house had reason to
be cautious. An escaped slave, she was a "conductor"—one who led slaves
out of bondage—on what was known as the Underground Railroad. And
she was one of the most extraordinary women in American history.

Harriet Tubman's home in Auburn, New York   (Cayuga County Historian)

Harriet Tubman (ca. 1820–1913) was born in about 1820 (there were no records kept of her birth) in squalid slave quarters on a plantation owned by Edward Brodas on the Eastern Shore in Maryland. Her name was Araminta Ross, daughter of slaves Ben Ross and Harriet Greene. Her parents, she later liked to recount, were both members of the Ashanti tribe of West Africa, a tribe known for its fierceness in conflict, a heritage she was proud of.

Araminta soon went by the nickname Minta during her childhood, but childhood didn't last long on the plantation. By the age of six she was put to work. Her first job was to carry water to the field hands, as well as to her father Ben and the other slaves cutting trees in the thick woods of the plantation. It was hard, backbreaking work that lasted sunup to sundown, but she preferred it to the times when she was hired out by the plantation owner. On these occasions, when the owner didn't need her, she had to go work on other plantations or in other white people's homes. Watching Minta being carried off, her mother Harriet, known as Old Rit, would dread the worst. Many people who hired slaves, she knew, were too poor to own slaves themselves, and they took malicious delight in humiliating and beating their hired slaves in order to feel superior.

Minta made her first attempt at escape after she was severely beaten by a white woman who had rented her from the slave owner Brodas. Minta hid, battered and nearly naked, in a pig trough for four days. Finally, ill and near starvation, she had to go back. Angry, the white woman returned her to the plantation complaining bitterly that she was not a good slave.

Minta was, however, independent minded, intelligent and strong. And, although she was only five feet tall even after she reached her teens, she convinced the master of the plantation that she could work in the fields and woods along with the strongest men. As she worked in the woods with her father Ben, she learned skills—how to read the signs of nature, follow animal trails and move quietly through the forest—that later would serve her well.

She worked hard alongside her father and learned a lot, although what she learned she kept well hidden. Things started to change when the plantation started to lose money. Now not just the troublemakers, or the so-called useless slaves, were being sold off, as had always been the custom, but, more and more, even working slaves were being sold and "sent South" each week. Minta knew in the Deep South the overseers were stricter and faster with the whip, the work was even more arduous and slaves' lives appreciably shorter. Watching men, women and children being gathered up like cattle, chained in groups and herded down the dusty roads that led away from the plantation, young Minta knew that she would soon be in one of those groups.

In fact she had already narrowly escaped being sold off. One day, when another slave had tried to run away, the angry overseer threw a heavy object after him. Unfortunately Minta—who may have been trying to help the escapee—got in the way and received a severe blow to the head that knocked her unconscious. For weeks she was in a coma, and when she finally came out, she later recalled seeing the plantation owner standing in the doorway, inquiring how she was. Was she well enough to sell? he wanted to know. But recovery was very slow and uncertain, and no one would buy her. For the rest of her life she suffered from sudden spells of lethargy and blackouts as a result of the injury.

In about 1844 she married a free black man named John Tubman, taking his name and by this time taking her mother's first name, Harriet. Despite her marriage, though, she was not allowed to spend the night in her husband's cabin. When she began to talk about trying to escape from her owner, her husband would have nothing to do with it. To make matters worse, he told her that if she did make the attempt he would inform the authorities.

But in 1849 her owner Brodas died, and many slaves were scheduled to be sold off. Since Harriet could never be sure when a seizure would hit, she knew that running for the border on her own would be difficult and dangerous. So one night, in spite of John Tubman's threat, she convinced three of her brothers to escape with her. Only a few miles into the woods, though, her brothers became frightened that they would be caught, and, unsure that they could find their way back alone, they forced her to return with them. After that she knew that there wasn't any choice. She would have to go alone.

"I had reasoned this one out in my mind," she remembered later. "There was one of two things I had a right to—liberty or death. If I could not have one, I could have the other, for no man could take me alive. I shall fight for me to go on. . . ."

So Harriet Tubman set out, alone and on foot, at the age of about 29. Bundling up a few possessions, she headed first to the home of a friendly white woman who had hinted in the past that she could be of help if it was ever needed. It was Harriet's first contact with the Underground Railroad—which, she quickly learned, was not a railroad at all, but a loosely organized network of people and safe houses. The system was secretly coordinated to help escaping slaves make their way from one house to another across the South to the northern states, Canada and freedom. The woman supplied names of others who would help, as well as places to go to find food, shelter and even aid in transportation. Tubman was on her way to freedom. Because the network operated in utmost secrecy, using the cover of darkness and disguise, it was referred to as "underground." And because its operation was done along carefully planned routes, it much resembled a railroad line. The safe houses—shelters or food stops along the way—were called "stations," the various routes themselves were called "lines" and the people who aided were called "conductors." Not all blacks who escaped from slavery in the South made use of the Underground Railroad—many managed alone and unaided, suffering great hardships along the way. But those who took advantage of the Railroad relied on its conductors for their safety.

Tubman's journey took her 90 miles on foot, through swamps and woods, to the Mason-Dixon line, the line between slave states and free states. "I had crossed the line of which I had been so long dreaming," she later recounted. "I was free, but there was no one there to welcome me to the land of freedom." She had crossed the border between Maryland, a slave state, and the free state of Pennsylvania. From then on, she said, "I was a stranger in a strange land, and my home after all was down in the old cabin quarter with the old folks, and my brothers and sisters." She would never look back, but she would go back, over and over again.

Harriet Tubman was about to become the most famous and daring of all the conductors of the Underground Railroad. She made the first of her many dangerous journeys back to the South in 1850. Working in Philadelphia, Pennsylvania, as a dishwasher and trying to save enough money to help the rest of her family flee north, she began visiting the office of the Philadelphia Vigilance Committee. The committee's president was a Quaker (member of the Society of Friends, a religious group believing in equality and nonviolence) named J. Miller McKim, and its secretary, a free African American named William Still. Both were active in the Underground Railroad. They and the rest of the committee offered their services any time of the day or night to escaping and escaped fugitives. Many fugitive slaves visited the office to obtain information about their relatives still in the South, looking for contacts with relatives in the North, or just exchanging information about jobs and adventures. Harriet heard through this active grapevine that one of her brothers-in-law, her sister and sister's children were about to be sold and shipped farther south to work in a chain gang. Immediately she volunteered to return to Maryland and lead them out via the Underground Railroad. It took some talking, but she convinced the committee that she not only would be able to accomplish the dangerous job but that her experience traveling by day and night through the woods made her the best person to do it.

Harriet Tubman (standing, left) with some of the slaves she freed (Sophia Smith Collection, Smith College)

She was the best. It was the first of 19 successful trips that she would make from the North to the South, personally leading out more than 300 fugitive slaves, at first bringing them to the safety of the Northern states. In that same year, a new Fugitive Slave Act was passed by the U.S. Congress, at the instigation of the Southern legislators. This act declared that all escaped slaves had to be returned to their Southern owners, making even the free states of the North unsafe. So, Tubman began taking fugitives even farther north, into Canada, moving her own home base from Auburn to Canada for a time as well. There she spent her winters, moving back to the States during the summers to work at odd jobs and make her dangerous trips into the South.

Tubman planned her trips ingeniously to avoid discovery and capture. She was a master of disguise, small and easily overlooked, sometimes with a red bandanna, sometimes dressed in men's clothing, sometimes a stooped woman in a bonnet. She foresaw every detail and never took the same route twice, using misinformation to confuse pursuers. Often she hired someone to follow behind the pursuing bands of slave catchers to tear down the "wanted" posters they put up. She usually met her charges in the woods, away from the plantations, so that if something went wrong at the outset, she wouldn't be compromised and could return another day to help another group of slaves. Once the group was formed, she kept strict discipline, and there was no turning back.

"Keep going," she would tell them. "Children, if you are tired, keep going; if you are scared, keep going; if you are hungry, keep going; if you want to taste freedom, keep going." But she backed up her words with more than rhetoric. She also carried a shotgun and made clear that she meant to use it on anyone intent on turning back or giving up. She never had to, but in later years, people often asked her if she really would have shot anyone. "If he was weak enough to give out," she replied, her eyes steely, "he'd be weak enough to betray us all, and all those who helped us; and do you think I'd let so many die for one coward . . .?"

Tubman began to make many friends and allies among abolitionists, including Frederick Douglass, William Lloyd Garrison and Charles Sumner. Among these was William H. Seward of Auburn, New York, former state governor, U.S. senator and future U.S. secretary of state (1861–69). Recognizing that she needed a place to settle down and have a sense of security, in 1857 Seward presented her with the deed to the wood-frame house now standing at 180 South Street. As later recounted by Tubman's biographer Sarah Bradford, Seward told Tubman, "Harriet, you have worked for others long enough." She bought the house from him on easy terms, and the small town of Auburn—one of the major stations along the route of the Underground Railroad—became her home for the rest of her life. In this house Harriet had places to hide and make quick getaways, as in any Underground Railroad station, but it's doubtful that Tubman ever took fugitive slaves there, since her place would have been the first place slave catchers would look. White families, such as the Sewards, could provide a safer haven.

During this same period, Tubman heard that her father Ben, now in his seventies and still a slave back in Maryland, had been caught helping a slave to escape. If found guilty for this extremely serious offense, he would receive severe punishment, even at his age. She sped south to the rescue. Moving under cover of night, she slipped back across the border and back across the swamps and woodlands of the Eastern Shore to her parents' cabin, where she woke her startled mother and father and quickly explained the plan. Then she slipped back out into the darkness, found a horse in the plantation stable, which she hitched to a dilapidated old wagon, and pulled up outside her parents' cabin. Both parents had belongings that they couldn't bear to part with—her mother wouldn't leave without her feather bed; her father couldn't leave behind his broadax and tools—so Harriet loaded those up, along with her parents, and set off for Wilmington, Delaware. Three days later, they arrived, unharmed, at the Underground Railroad station run by Quaker Thomas Garrett. "I furnished her with money to take them all to Canada," Garrett later wrote. "I afterward sold their horse and sent them the balance of the proceeds."

The harsh Canadian winter, though, was hard on the elderly couple, and seeing that few people in the North were complying any longer with the Fugitive Slave Act, Tubman decided to take a chance. So she and her parents moved to the wood-frame house in Auburn, where they lived with her until their deaths in the 1870s, both nearly 100 years old.

Meanwhile, with a huge $40,000 reward offered by Southern slaveholders for her capture, and her reputation among slaves as "Moses, the deliverer," Tubman inevitably became legendary to Northern abolitionists. So it was no surprise in 1858–59 when one of the most famous and controversial abolitionists of them all, John Brown, met with her a couple of times in Boston where she was on a speaking tour. During those visits Harriet drew up maps for Brown, describing the various escape routes and hiding places she knew that led out of the South and into the Northern states. In his letters Brown referred to her as "one of the best and bravest persons on this continent—*General* Tubman as we call her." Brown's letters also reveal that he expected Harriet might join him in the raid he planned on the federal arsenal at Harper's Ferry, Virginia (now Harpers Ferry, W. Va.) Brown believed that this raid, if successful, would provide inspiration to slaves in the South, and he hoped to see a general insurrection among Southern blacks. But Harriet, possibly for reasons of illness, did not join up with Brown and his men. The raid took place on October 16, 1859, but failed. Defeated by federal troops, the raiders fled, but Brown and six of his followers were hunted down and hanged. Had Tubman been there, some historians conjecture, it might have gone differently. "It is difficult," wrote Louis Filler in 1974, "to believe she would have permitted herself to be penned up in the arsenal, as Brown was, and subjected to military assault and trial."

With the outbreak of the Civil War in 1861, Tubman's work with the Underground Railroad came to an end. During its years of operation, a total of some 40,000 to 100,000 slaves had escaped using the complex network of the Railroad. But the fight for black freedom was far from over, and Harriet Tubman was not through fighting. Volunteering her services, she spent three years nursing the sick and wounded in Florida and the Carolinas and worked as a scout and spy under the command of Colonel James Montgomery. The information that she was able to collect behind Southern lines aided Montgomery in his successful raids in the Southern coastal areas, including his most daring expedition up the Combahee River in June 1863. Guided by Tubman, who traveled right along with him, Montgomery and his detachment of 300 black soldiers successfully freed more than 800 slaves and led them to safety.

Tubman returned to Auburn and her parents after the war. She was nearly destitute, but she never stopped helping people. Although she never received any schooling, she tirelessly raised money for black schools. She also raised money to help former slaves, destitute children, the hungry and the sick. She welcomed former slaves into her home. She gave talks about the rights of African Americans and spoke out for women's rights.

During the postwar years, Sarah Bradford, an Auburn writer, became interested in Tubman and wrote her biography *Scenes in the Life of Harriet Tubman*, which was first published in 1869 and came out in a revision in 1886 as *Harriet Tubman: The Moses of Her People*. Bradford gave Tubman the entire proceeds from the book, amounting to $1,200, a very large sum at the time. This enabled Tubman to meet her expenses and have some left over for feeding hungry strangers and giving money to schools for blacks.

One of those who appeared at Tubman's door in 1869 was a young man of about 25 named Nelson Davis. She had met Davis in 1860 in South Carolina, on an army base where he served in the Union army during the war, a private in Company G of the Eighth U.S. Colored Infantry Volunteers. Davis now asked Tubman to marry him, and she accepted. They were married before friends, both black and white, on March 18, 1869. In its coverage of the story, the Auburn newspaper noted jubilantly,

"Both born slaves . . . they stood there, last evening, *free*, and were joined as man and wife."

Unfortunately Davis, who was 24 years younger than Harriet, had contracted tuberculosis during his service in the army and was never well afterward. Harriet supported them both by selling vegetables from her garden, peddling door to door to wealthy neighbors in Auburn. Neighbors were always glad to see her. As one of them later recalled, "Harriet when I knew her in her matriarchal phase was a magnificent-looking woman, true African, with a broad nose, very black, and of medium height. I used to often sit and listen to her stories when I could get her to tell them." Nelson Davis lived with Harriet for 19 years, until he died in 1888. He was only 44.

Although the military expressed appreciation for Tubman's services during the war, the U.S. government never paid her for any of the work that she

The state historical marker at Tubman's home   (Cayuga County Historian)

did. However, thanks to Davis's time of service, as the widow of a veteran she was finally awarded a pension of $8 a month in 1890, increased to $20 a month in 1899. This income greatly improved her finances, and finally, with the help of the African Methodist Episcopal Zion Church, she was able to transform her house in 1908 into a home for aged and destitute blacks. By now in her eighties or nineties, she spent her last days in the Auburn house recounting stories of the Underground Railroad to visitors who came to listen as she and other residents rocked their chairs in the shade on the wide veranda.

In a letter to Harriet written in 1868, Frederick Douglass spoke eloquently of her extraordinary contribution, for which he felt she had never received enough recognition:

> The midnight sky and the silent stars have been the witnesses of your devotion to freedom and your heroism. Excepting John Brown . . . I know of no one who has willingly encountered more perils and hardships to serve our enslaved people than you have.

A fearless fighter for the cause of freedom, Tubman had never hesitated to risk her life for the rights of African Americans. Throughout her life Harriet Tubman bore the scars of slavery, and yet she always stood by her people, even when it meant she had to face mortal danger or break the law to do so. In her lifetime the greatest recognition of the magnitude of her deeds came in 1897, when Queen Victoria of England, moved by Sarah Bradford's biography, sent Tubman a silver medal. Friends said Tubman fingered the letter that came with it until it was "worn to a shadow."

Harriet Tubman died of pneumonia in her wood-frame house in Auburn on March 10, 1913. Local veterans of the Civil War gave her a military burial in Fort Hill Cemetery in Auburn. A year later, on July 13, 1914, in an unprecedented salute, the city of Auburn declared a city-wide memorial day, placing a plaque in her memory at the county courthouse. Booker T. Washington spoke at the ceremony. In 1978 the U.S. government issued a stamp in her honor.

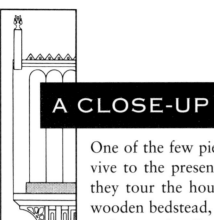

A CLOSE-UP | A PLACE TO REST

One of the few pieces of Harriet Tubman's furniture to survive to the present is her bed, which visitors can see when they tour the house at 180 South Street. Here, on the tall wooden bedstead, her shawl still hangs, as if ready for her to pick up and pull around her shoulders against the cool night air. This bed, though plain and small, must have seemed a wonderful resting place to the woman who had slept in ditches, on barn floors, in attics and pig sties over the years.

Harriet Tubman's bed   (Cayuga County Historian)

Pictures taken even in her later years continued to show the steely determination in her eyes, the fighting spirit and unflinching will that had always set her apart. Her courageous motto, "I can't die but once," had seen her through many a harrowing moment, until finally, on March 10, 1913, Harriet Tubman closed those spirited eyes for the last time. Friends gathered round her bed, singing "Swing Low, Sweet Chariot." Today, standing at her bedside, visitors can imagine the low, murmuring sounds as their voices lift and swell into the music of the great spiritual that she loved so well.

PRESERVING IT FOR THE FUTURE

In 1908, Harriet Tubman's wood-frame house was moved to its present location and, with the financial and management aid of the African Methodist Episcopal Zion Church, Harriet Tubman transformed the house into a home for aged and indigent blacks. However it continued to operate for only a year following her death. From 1914 until 1947 the house was unused and fell into disrepair. The passageways and tunnels built for use by runaway slaves had caved in and had to be closed up for safety, and much of the furniture had been stolen. In 1947, the African Methodist Episcopal Zion Church began renovating the structure, and much of the furniture was replaced with donations of pieces from the period that are typical of the sparse furniture Harriet Tubman once had in her home. In 1932 the site became a New York State Historic Site, and in 1974 it became designated a National Historic Landmark, while continuing under the management of the African Methodist Episcopal Zion Churches of the Western New York Conference.

EXPLORING ◆ FURTHER

Readings about Harriet Tubman and the Underground Railroad

Blockson, Charles L. *The Underground Railroad*. New York: Prentice-Hall, 1987.

Bradford, Sarah. *Harriet Tubman: The Moses of Her People*. 1886. Reprinted, Secaucus, N.J: Citadel Press, 1974.

Campbell, Stanley W. *The Slave Catchers: Enforcement of the Fugitive Slave Law, 1850–1860*. Chapel Hill: University of North Carolina Press, 1968

Conrad, Earl. *Harriet Tubman*. Washington, D.C.: Associated Publishers, Erickson, 1942.

Davidson, Nancy A. "Harriet Tubman, Underground Railroad Conductor," *Epic Lives: One Hundred Black Women Who Made a Difference*, edited by Jessie Carney Smith. Detroit: Visible Ink Press, 1993.

Gara, Larry. *The Liberty Line: The Legend of the Underground Railroad*. Lexington: University of Kentucky Press, 1961.

Petry, Ann. *Harriet Tubman: Conductor on the Underground Railroad*. New York: Thomas Y. Crowell and Co., 1955.

Still, William. *The Underground Railroad*. Chicago: Johnson Publications, Inc., 1970.

Taylor, M. W. *Harriet Tubman. Antislavery Activist*. Black Americans of Achievement Series. Broomall, Pa.: Chelsea House Publishers, 1994.

Related Places

Seward House
33 South Street
Auburn, NY 13021
(315) 252-1283

Home of William Henry and Frances Seward. The last stop on Harriet Tubman's vegetable run; here she typically would sit in a rocking chair in the kitchen and fall asleep. The Seward house was also an Underground Railroad stop, hiding fugitives in a large storage area above the carriage house, which was connected to the main house. In addition to many other items of historical interest, artifacts connected with Tubman are on display.

Levi Coffin House
North Main Street
Fountain City, IN 47341
(317) 847-2432

A Quaker white man who left North Carolina in protest against the increasingly stringent black codes, Levi Coffin and his wife arrived in Newport (now Fountain City), Indiana in 1826. This house became a hub of the Underground Railroad in several surrounding states. In their 20 years there, the Coffins helped about 2,000 men, women and children escape to freedom, moving later to Cincinnati, Ohio, where they helped about 1,100 more. The restored Coffin house is open to visitors, who can see the hidden quarters for runaways and witness the past brought to life by historical interpreters.

John Rankin House State Memorial
1824 Liberty Hall
Ripley, OH 45167
(513) 392-1627

The first stop across the Ohio River from Tennessee on the way to freedom in Canada, Reverend John Rankin's house provided a haven for those evading the slave catchers along the river. He and his wife Jean founded the American Anti-Slavery Society here in 1828, and they helped approximately 2,000 individuals flee the bonds of slavery. Visitors can tour the home, as well as view the cellar beneath the barn and a hiding place in the attic, both used to hide fugitives.

Booker T. Washington
National Monument

BIRTHPLACE OF AN EDUCATOR
Hardy, Virginia

AT A GLANCE

Built: ca. 1840, reconstructed 1957

Birthplace of Booker T. Washington, civil rights activist and educator

A reconstruction of the Burroughs farm, where Booker T. Washington spent
the first nine years of his life. A National Monument, the farm is run by the
National Park Service. The 224-acre park contains most of the original 207
acres of the Burroughs plantation and a replica of Washington's
birthplace, a cabin measuring 12-by-16 feet.

Address:

Booker T. Washington National Monument
Route 3, Box 310, Highway 122, Hardy, VA 24101, (703) 721-2094

On this small tobacco farm in central Virginia, a young black slave fed the hogs, carried water and fanned flies from the table while his master's family ate. From this early life of poverty and illiteracy, Booker T. Washington, freed, became an educator, philosopher, advisor and influential statesman.

> To those of my race who depend on bettering their condition
> in a foreign land, or who underestimate the importance of
> cultivating friendly relations with the Southern white man,
> who is their next door neighbor, I would say: "Cast down
> your bucket where you are"—cast it down in making
> friends in every manly way of the people of all races
> by whom we are surrounded.
>
> —Booker T. Washington, 1895 at the Cotton States
> International Exposition in Atlanta

♦ ♦ ♦ ♦ ♦

For nine-year-old Booker Taliaferro Washington (1856–1915), growing up on the Burroughs plantation meant growing up in a world of limitations. He carried books to school for the daughter of plantation owner James Burroughs and brought back the horse for a day in the fields. He could go to the school grounds, but it was against the law for him to receive an education.

"I was never permitted to go farther than the schoolroom door . . . ," he later wrote. "From the moment that it was made clear to me that I was not to go to school, that it was dangerous for me to learn to read, from that moment I resolved that I should never be satisfied until I learned what this dangerous practice was like."

The Booker T. Washington National Monument is a restoration of the modest mid-19th-century farm owned by the couple James and Elizabeth Burroughs. Not all Southern plantations were vast—and by no means were all slave owners wealthy. Here Washington was born to the plantation cook, a black woman. His father was a white man from a nearby farm. Unfortunately none of the original buildings remains from Washington's time, but several of the cabins and outbuildings have been reconstructed; the sites of other buildings are indicated by markers. Fields are defined by split-rail fences, just as they were in Washington's time there.

As Washington recalled, "The cabin was without glass windows [and] only had openings in the side to let in light and also the cold, chilly air of winter." The interior, which doubled as a kitchen for the master's house, has been re-created to reflect Washington's description in his autobiography—dirt floor, whitewashed walls, a rough table and bench, and crude shelves, pots, fireplace tools and a root cellar, which Booker called a "potato hole." There are no beds. Washington and his brother and sister slept bundled in rags for warmth, on the dirt floor.

Washington recalled meals for slaves on the plantation as haphazard. "On the plantation in Virginia," he wrote, "and even later, meals were

Reconstruction of the cabin where Booker T. Washington was born   (Courtesy of the National Park Service)

gotten by the children very much as dumb animals get theirs." Occasionally he would find a scrap of meat or a potato. Later he might get a cup of milk or a piece of bread. The most common elements of his childhood diet were pork and corn bread. "I cannot remember a single instance during my childhood or early boyhood," he recalled, "when . . . the family ate in a civilized manner."

The plantation was neither large nor elegant. The "big house" in which Booker sometimes worked fanning flies was really little more than a five-room log farmhouse. And the farm wasn't well kept—because the Burroughs owned only 10 slaves and only 2 of those were adult males. "Fences were out of repair," Washington recalled, "gates were hanging half off the hinges, doors creaked, window-panes were out, plastering had fallen but was not replaced, weeds grew in the yard." As visitors tour the premises, they can see the corncrib, horse barn, chicken lot, smokehouse, blacksmith shed and tobacco barn, all much as they were when young Booker lived there.

The Burroughs were shorthanded, so unlike owners of larger plantations, they toiled beside their slaves in the field and they got to know them. But the Burroughs still thought of their slaves as property, listed alongside animals in a catalog of their possessions. In their 1861 listing of this kind, a little boy named simply Booker was valued at $400. Little did they know that this same Booker would one day be valued very differently, remembered and respected for his work promoting education among African Americans.

Young Washington could not remember a time when he was ever idle. Even as a child he was kept busy, carrying water from the spring to his mother in the kitchen, cleaning the yards, carrying water to the men in the fields or taking corn to be ground at the mill 3 miles away.

In 1865 the Civil War ended and slaves were set free. A Union officer stood on the steps of the Burroughs house and read the Emancipation Proclamation to the assembled Burroughs slaves. In part he read the following words: "And by virtue of the power, and for the purpose aforesaid, I do order and declare that all persons held as slaves within said designated States, are and hence forward shall be free."

Washington later recounted that his mother leaned over, once the reading was finished, and kissed all her children, explaining tearfully that "this

From this spring, young Booker carried water to his mother in the log cabin. (Courtesy of the National Park Service)

was the day for which she had been so long praying, but fearing that she would never live to see."

At the time of emancipation, Booker T. Washington was an illiterate nine-year-old boy who had been a slave all his life. He left behind him the only life he knew—slavery and this farm. But, always perceiving the favorable, looking back he would recount,

> When freedom came, the slaves were almost as well fitted to begin life anew as the master, except in the matter of book-learning and ownership of property. The slave owner and his sons had mastered no special industry. They unconsciously had imbibed the feeling that manual labor was not the proper thing for them. On the other hand, the slaves, in many cases had mastered some handicraft, and none was ashamed, and few unwilling, to labor.

Now free, Washington's mother decided to try to rejoin his father, who worked in a salt mine in West Virginia, and so the family set off, with the children traveling on foot. Once they arrived in West Virginia, young Booker began working in the salt mines and later the coal mines. Determined to learn how to read, he taught himself the alphabet and then resolved to attend school, even if it meant working from 4:00 A.M., until 9:00 A.M. when school started, and then returning to the mine after school. Asked for his last name at school, he chose Washington, not knowing that his mother had named him Booker Taliaferro [TAL-yuh-FAIR-roh]. After he learned that, he went by Booker Taliaferro Washington.

Within a few years Booker was taken on as a houseboy by a wealthy townswoman who further encouraged his desire for learning. He resolved in 1872 to gain entrance to Hampton Institute, in the town of Hampton in southeast Virginia, one of the few schools in the country where African Americans could pursue a higher education. To get there, he left his job and walked nearly 500 miles, arriving dirty, ragged looking and haggard. His request for admission to Hampton was at first looked on without enthusiasm, but he gained entrance by offering to do janitorial work to pay the fees. "At Hampton," he later wrote, "I not only learned that it was not a disgrace to labor, but learned to love labor, not alone for its financial value, but for labor's own sake and for the independence and self-reliance which the ability to do something which the world wants done brings."

Booker T. *Washington*   (Courtesy of the National Park Service)

BOOKER T. WASHINGTON NATIONAL MONUMENT

Graduating in 1875, he so distinguished himself as a student that he was chosen in 1881 to head a new school for blacks, Tuskegee Institute in Alabama. The school began in a run-down church with 30 students, but within a few years, it had a $2 million endowment and 1,500 students. Twenty years after its founding, the institution owned 2,300 acres of land, with more than 700 acres under cultivation each year, entirely using student labor. The campus was dotted with some 40 buildings, all of them built using student talent and skills. Washington's educational philosophy at Tuskegee maintained that students should learn practical skills as well as other subjects.

But, while he was praised for his ability as an administrator and effective educator at Tuskegee Institute, Washington has also come under harsh criticism as an African American who accommodated white segregation policies and discrimination when he should have allied himself with his people against these injustices. Some people feel that he opportunistically let issues go by when it was more convenient to do so, instead of speaking out against the racial violence and oppression of his day. More militant African Americans opposed his quiescent tactics and spoke out against him.

In 1895 Washington gave a speech called "The Atlanta Compromise," in which he gained popularity among white listeners for encouraging economic progress without challenging racial segregation. During this speech he outlined his philosophy of self-help and cooperation between blacks and whites. "Cast down your bucket where you are," he admonished African Americans, "and accommodate."

Another key figure in African-American education, W. E. B. DuBois [doo-BOYZ], spoke out in direct opposition to many of Washington's educational premises. Washington, thought DuBois, was playing into the hands of Jim Crow laws with his emphasis on vocational education. A young historian and Harvard College graduate, DuBois, by contrast, recommended that all African Americans should be uplifted by a select few gifted black intellectuals. DuBois referred to this elite group as the Talented Tenth, estimating that they made up about a 10th of the African-American population. In 1905, with other black intellectuals, he formed a group called the Niagara Movement, calling for full citizenship rights for all blacks and public recognition for their contributions to American strength and progress. It was the nucleus of the group that eventually came to be called the National Association for the Advancement of Colored People (NAACP).

In later years Washington moved away from his accommodationist policies. In 1915 he joined other black leaders in protesting the stereotypical portrayal of blacks in the movie *Birth of a Nation*, and he spoke out more frankly against racism.

In 1908, when Booker T. Washington returned to visit his boyhood home at age 43, he was president of Tuskegee Institute, a respected college (now Tuskegee University). He had made the school a major center for industrial and agricultural training, had become a well-known public speaker on issues of education and race relations and had earned a reputation as a statesman and influential activist. "I want to emphasize the fact," he said at that time, "that during all the time I have been absent, I have never forgotten this spot. I have never forgotten the impression made upon my life. I have never forgotten those who owned me as a slave boy here."

Washington received an honorary degree from Harvard University and was an adviser on interracial issues to three presidents, William McKinley, Theodore Roosevelt and William Howard Taft. His autobiography, *Up from Slavery*, published in 1901, was one of 13 books that he wrote.

Washington was in New York City when he fell ill in November 1915. With the realization that he was dying, he sped homeward to the South, where he had lived all his life. Booker T. Washington died at Tuskegee, Alabama, in 1915, and he is buried on the Tuskegee University campus. He continues to be remembered for his work helping African Americans overcome the economic oppression that continued to enslave them long after the Emancipation Proclamation established their freedom as citizens. And he is remembered as a man who overcame, like Frederick Douglass and Harriet Tubman, the legacy of birth in slavery—a beginning that for him took place in a tiny, shabby cabin that doubled as a kitchen for the plantation where his mother lived.

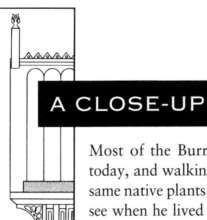

A CLOSE-UP

FARMING IN THE VIRGINIA PIEDMONT

Most of the Burroughs acreage was undeveloped, as it is today, and walking along the trails, visitors can see much the same native plants and small animals that young Booker could see when he lived there. The portion of the acreage that was improved was divided up by zigzag, split-rail fencing, still there today, which separated the areas used for crops from those for grazing the livestock. Most of the farm's income came from about 5 acres of tobacco planting, but some other crops were grown for use on the farm, including flax, which the women wove into rough cloth for garments. Corn, wheat and oats were also grown and stored in open cribs and used as livestock feed or ground into meal.

In the Deep South, cotton was king, but in the Virginia Piedmont area, the cash crop that grew best was tobacco. Its cultivation required intensive labor, though—one of the reasons why the Bur-roughs family could barely scratch out a living.

The farm had a blacksmith shed, as well, where the necessities of farm life were

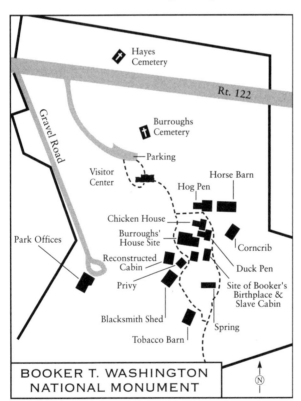

Map of the farm, Booker T. Washington National Monument

forged—although the shop in town provided iron tools and carried out major repairs. Slaves undertook minor projects and small carpentry jobs here, however. Farm workers also manufactured soap, candles, baskets and shakes for shingles, which constantly needed replacing.

PRESERVING IT FOR THE FUTURE

Authorized by Congress on April 2, 1956, Booker T. Washington National Monument became a reality in June 1957. Officially, the park was set aside as "A memorial to Booker T. Washington, noted negro educator and apostle of good will." The Burroughs farm gives a very different impression from Tara, the plantation in *Gone with the Wind*. It provides an opportunity to show firsthand what slavery was and what it did to human beings, both black and white.

The park provides a replicated cultural landscape integrated with a partially reconstructed plantation farmstead, a visitor center with exhibits, additional exhibits on the farm and a nature trail. Hiking trails include the Plantation Trail, a .25 mile loop through the historic area, and the Jack-O-Lantern Branch Trail, which leads through the fields and woodlands for 1.5 miles, where deer, fox, rabbit and other small animals can be seen along the trail.

At the visitor center museum, one can also view *Longing to Learn*, the award-winning 15-minute slide program, and there one can also see speech manuscripts handwritten by Washington.

EXPLORING ◆ FURTHER

Readings by and about Booker T. Washington

Harlan, Louis. *Booker T. Washington: The Making of a Black Leader*. New York: Oxford University Press, 1972.

———. *Booker T. Washington: The Wizard of Tuskegee, 1901–1915.* New York: Oxford University Press, 1984.

Schroeder, Alan. *Booker T. Washington: Educator and Racial Spokesman.* Black Americans of Achievement series. Broomall, Pa.: Chelsea Publishers, 1992.

Washington, Booker T. *Up from Slavery.* New York: Doubleday, 1901.

Readings by W. E. B. DuBois

DuBois, W. E. B. *The Souls of Black Folk.* Scarborough, Ontario: New American Library of Canada, Ltd., 1969.

Related Places

Tuskegee Institute National Historic Site
399 Old Montgomery Road
Tuskegee, AL 36088
(334) 727-6390

Founded by Booker T. Washington, this was the first institution of higher learning dedicated to vocational training for blacks. The buildings of this institute were built of bricks made by students.

Colonial Williamsburg
P.O. Box 1776
1 Visitor Center Drive
Williamsburg, VA 23185
(800)-HISTORY

More than half the colonial population was black, and their abilities and contributions were essential to the success of the colony at Williamsburg. Visitors to Williamsburg can take tours—called "The Other Half Tours"— which cover the life and involvement of slaves in Williamsburg.

Nicodemus, Kansas

SETTLEMENT BUILT BY EARLY EXODUSTERS
Nicodemus, Kansas

AT A GLANCE

Built: 1877

All-black community settled in Western Kansas in the 1870s.

Now the home of some 60 people, Nicodemus, Kansas,
was originally established as an all-black settlement, peopled by former
slaves from Kentucky and Tennessee—a precursor of the Exoduster
Movement of the years 1879–81.

Address:

Nicodemus National Historical Landmark,
U.S. Highway 24, 2 miles west of the Rooks-Graham County line

Mailing Address:

c/o Nicodemus Colony Historical Society, R.R. 2, Box 139
Bogue, KS 67625
(913) 421-3311

> *It would be the land of Canaan, the settlers believed, made free of racial conflict by John Brown before the Civil War; a land of milk and honey; the promised land.*

When we got in sight of Nicodemus, the men shouted, "There is Nicodemus!" Being very sick, I hailed this news with gladness. I looked with all the eyes I had. "Where is Nicodemus? I don't see it." My husband pointed out various smokes coming out the ground and said, "That is Nicodemus." The families lived in dugouts. We landed and once again struck tents. The scenery . . . was not at all inviting, and I began to cry.

—Willianna Hickman, Nicodemus settler, 1878

♦ ♦ ♦ ♦ ♦

The A.M.E. Church, ca. 1943   (William T. Belleau. The Nicodemus Historical Society)

As Reconstruction faded and restrictions against former slaves increased in the states of the former Confederacy, several groups of blacks migrating to Kansas founded the town of Nicodemus on the Solomon River. The large number of blacks leaving the South was called the Great Exodus, and the settlers Exodusters. The settlers who founded Nicodemus were the early wave of a major migration that hit Kansas between 1879 and 1881—some 6,000 Exodusters, freed people from Louisiana, Mississippi, Texas and other southern states who responded to the leadership of Henry Adams and Benjamin "Pap" Singleton, who encouraged fellow African Americans to move west, in search of a better life, freer and, they believed less encumbered by racial prejudice. Many might rather have gone to Liberia, the colony some African Americans were founding in Africa. But it cost a lot less money to go to Kansas, and the place seemed more appealing than the South, where white terrorism began to reign after the end of Reconstruction in 1877. Many blacks began to fear a return to a type of slavery. Others were just discouraged, as one man told a reporter in 1879, "We've been working for 14 long years, and we ain't no better off than we was when we commenced." Meanwhile Southern whites, worried about a labor shortage, tried to prevent their departure, probably only adding further momentum to the movement.

As for Kansas, at the outset, the Missouri Compromise of 1820 had prohibited slavery in the Kansas Territory, although this stand was weakened by the Compromise of 1850 and then revoked by the Kansas-Nebraska Act of 1850. Yet African Americans remembered that John Brown, who by the 1870s had become a legend, had reportedly cleaned slavery out of Kansas before the Civil War. Some 60,000 African Americans are believed to have left the South for Kansas between 1875 and 1881. Most settled in urban areas, such as Topeka or Kansas City.

For some, the possibility of land ownership in Kansas loomed large as a very real attraction. Anyone with a filing fee of $10 could claim 160 acres of public land under the federal Homestead Act of 1862. After five years of working the land, a homesteader would then gain title. It seemed like a dream come true.

Posters circulated by land agents invited African Americans to leave their homes in the South to settle in Kansas. "All colored people that want to go to Kansas, . . . can do so for $5," promised the fliers for the black township of Nicodemus. Families packed up their belongings and headed west with high hopes. When they arrived, however, they found that the appeal of Nicodemus had been vastly overstated by its promoters.

Located on the southeastern border of Graham County on the high plains of northwestern Kansas, Nicodemus was an uncommonly bleak, treeless area. As one pioneer who witnessed the arrival of some immigrants recalled: "They finally reached their goal, a prairie quarter section, just north of the Solomon River—just plain prairie country—no horses, no wells, no shelter of any kind, and winter setting in." Between 1877 and 1878, some 600 or 700 people came to Nicodemus, 538 of them from Kentucky.

For protection against the bitter prairie winter, they dug their homes into the ground, carving dugout trenches 4 to 6 feet deep and 14 to 15 feet wide. They used sod to build their roofs, stacked atop a structure of tree branches. In the winter these makeshift roofs leaked profusely, and in the summer they harbored rodents and insects. As later depicted by an 1879 newspaper article, the typical sod house was:

> . . . roofed with poles and brush, with a covering of earth sufficient to keep out the rain. As lumber floors were regarded as an unnecessary luxury, all the lumber required was for a door and its frame, and one window. A fireplace at one end, in most cases, takes the place of a stove, and serves the double purpose of heating and cooking.

The walls of the house, barely extending above the ground, were made of bricks cut out of the sod, measuring 12 by 14 inches. These were usually laid in two rows in a staggered pattern held together by header bricks across the rows. Later a limestone wash was applied to the outside to repel water.

Of those arriving the second year, one entire group camped one night, turned around in discouragement and headed directly back. Far from being a land of milk and honey, Nicodemus was barren and unwelcoming. Many who left Nicodemus headed for Liberia instead. A few white settlers came, but the town remained predominantly black. It did not, however, realize its promise. Few came, and most who came didn't stay. The high point of the town's population was 700 in 1878, with many of the residents still living in sod houses, which were reputedly cool in sum-

All Colored People

THAT WANT TO

GO TO KANSAS,

On September 5th, 1877,

Can do so for $5.00

IMMIGRATION.

WHEREAS, We, the colored people of Lexington, Ky,. knowing that there is an abundance of choice lands now belonging to the Government, have assembled ourselves together for the purpose of locating on said lands. Therefore,

BE IT RESOLVED, That we do now organize ourselves into a Colony, as follows:— Any person wishing to become a member of this Colony can do so by paying the sum of one dollar ($1.00), and this money is to be paid by the first of September, 1877, in instalments of twenty-five cents at a time, or otherwise as may be desired.

RESOLVED, That this Colony has agreed to consolidate itself with the Nicodemus Towns, Solomon Valley, Graham County, Kansas, and can only do so by entering the vacant lands now in their midst, which costs $5.00.

RESOLVED, That this Colony shall consist of seven officers—President, Vice-President, Secretary, Treasurer, and three Trustees. President—M. M. Bell; Vice-President —Isaac Talbott; Secretary—W. J. Niles; Treasurer—Daniel Clarke; Trustees—Jerry Lee, William Jones, and Abner Webster.

RESOLVED, That this Colony shall have from one to two hundred militia, more or less, as the case may require, to keep peace and order, and any member failing to pay in his dues, as aforesaid, or failing to comply with the above rules in any particular, will not be recognized or protected by the Colony.

Handbill for attracting black settlers to Nicodemus, 1877   (The Kansas State Historical Society, Topeka, Kansas)

mer and warm in winter, but dark and depressing to live in. It was scarcely a better life than the one they left behind. Yet the settlers strove to make this home. In the words of a contemporary account describing one of the houses in Nicodemus:

> Inside it was very dark, and there were some cheap pictures on the walls. . . . There was a pile of cornstalks near the door, the favorite fuel of Nicodemus. In the space about the house were numerous chicken coops, made of corn stalks, and in front were marigolds and bachelors' buttons and four-o'clocks.

The town tried several times to attract a railroad and, in anticipation of the day when the railroad would surely arrive, enjoyed a period of growth in the spring of 1886, when success seemed imminent. Also, rains had been scarce in the early 1880s, making farming difficult. But by 1884, the rains had returned and farming was much better. In July 1886, the *Nicodemus Western Cyclone* expressed the general air of optimism, boasting:

> Nicodemus, the second town in size in the county, was originally settled by the colored race, and by their patience and untiring energy have succeeded in gaining a grand glorious victory over nature and the elements, and what used to be the Great American Desert, now blooms with waving grain. The period of suffering that once characterized this country is passed and peace and plenty reigns.

But the death knell came in 1888 when the railroad passed, not through Nicodemus, but through a neighboring town called Bogue. It was a blow from which the town could not recover. Although the dugouts had become sod buildings above ground and then structures of limestone, now people actually moved buildings out of Nicodemus to Bogue. Shopkeepers pulled up stakes and left. The newspaper editor left, even while he exhorted others to stay. Although at one time the town of Nicodemus had boasted a bank, livery stables, law offices, schools and a doctor, now the population steadily declined.

Some residents continued to hold to the roots they had put down, however. While white settlers had come during more prosperous years and then left when times got tough, a few black residents refused to give up. In the 1930s dust storms plagued Nicodemus as they did the rest of the Great

Nicodemus, Kansas, ca. 1885   (The Kansas State Historical Society, Topeka, Kansas)

Plains. Longtime resident Alvin Bates described farming his land north of Nicodemus during the 1930s, "I remember all the bad years. During the dirty thirties, we couldn't raise nothing. It wasn't the fact that we didn't get any rain, it was . . . the dust . . ."

Alvin's wife, Ada, added:

> I remember well the first dust storm that I seen. It was all black in the northwest, Billie over here was a little baby. And we had to cover her up with a wet sheet in her bed to keep her from choking to death. The dust was that thick in the house. Of course, we didn't have nothing but lamps in them days. You'd have to light the lamps right in the daytime because it was so dark.

But Nicodemus survived even this supreme test, which chased out many other farm families who had settled in the Midwest. By 1978, the number of residents had increased from low points in the 1930s to 100. Today, although the residents have dwindled to about 58, the town still survives, now with paved streets, buried telephone and electrical wiring, a playground, public park, rest area and other facilities.

Visitors to Nicodemus can tour the four remaining historic buildings: the African Methodist Episcopal Church, the First Baptist Church, the one-room school and the Fletcher House Hotel (also known as the St. Francis Hotel). Still the site of an annual summer Homecoming-Emancipation Celebration, begun in the 1870s, the town continues to stand as a monument to a group of people that, to be free of oppression, would rather leave the green beauty of Kentucky for the flat, arid, treeless landscape of the Kansas prairie. Of the several communities founded in this way in Kansas—Dunlap, Singleton and Nicodemus—only Nicodemus remains.

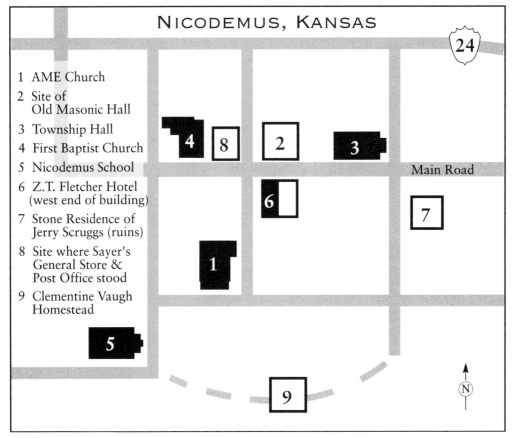

Historical Nicodemus

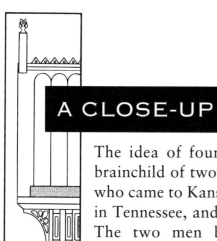

A CLOSE-UP | THE NAME OF THE PROMISED LAND

The idea of founding the town of Nicodemus was the brainchild of two men, W. H. Smith, a black entrepreneur who came to Kansas looking for land for a group of people in Tennessee, and W. R. Hill, a white town-site promoter. The two men became associated sometime between September 1876 and April 1877. Hill possessed the skills needed for promoting newly formed towns, and Smith had connections to blacks who were interested in coming to Kansas. They formed the Nicodemus Town Company on April 18, 1877, with Smith as president and Hill as treasurer.

No one is sure exactly how the two men came up with the name Nicodemus. Maybe, knowing the religious inclination of leaders of the group they were trying to attract, they chose the name of Nicodemus from the Biblical story about the man who became a secret follower of Jesus and helped bury him after the crucifixion. More likely, though, they had in mind the African prince Nicodemus, who was brought to the American colonies in 1692, where he was sold as a slave. He became famous as the first slave to buy his freedom in America, and he pledged that white people would some-day regret enslaving black people.

This story is borne out by a circular dated July 2, 1877. At the bottom of the handbill appeared a song glorifying Nicodemus, both man and town:

Nicodemus

Nicodemus was a slave of African birth,
And was bought for a bag full of gold;
He was reckoned a part of the salt of the earth,
But he died years ago, very old.

Nicodemus was a prophet, at least he was as wise,
For he told of the battles to come:
How we trembled with fear, when he rolled up his eyes,
And we heeded the shake of this thumb.

Chorus:

Good time coming, good time coming,
Long, long time on the way:
Run and tell Elija to hurry up the Pomp,
To meet us under the cottonwood tree,
In the Great Solomon Valley
At the first break of day.

PRESERVING IT FOR THE FUTURE

Recognizing that the town of Nicodemus did not have the human resources or funds to restore the historic structures, in 1974 the Afro-American Bicentennial Corporation prepared a historic district nomination for the National Register of Historic Places. In 1976 Nicodemus was designated a National Historic Landmark. In 1996 legislation was introduced to establish the historic district as a National Historic Site and incorporate it into the National Park Service.

EXPLORING ◆ FURTHER

Readings about Nicodemus and African-American Pioneers

Athearn, Robert. *In Search of Canaan: Black Migration to Kansas, 1879–80.* Lawrence: University Press of Kansas, 1978.

Chu, Daniel, and Bill Shaw. *Going Home to Nicodemus: The Story of an African American Frontier Town and the Pioneers Who Settled It.* New York: Julian Messner, 1995.

Katz, William Loren. *The Black West*. New York: Simon & Schuster, 1996.
———. *Black Women of the Old West*. New York, Atheneum, 1995.
Painter, Nell. *Exodusters: Black Migration to Kansas after Reconstruction*. Lawrence: University Press of Kansas, 1986.
U.S. Department of the Interior, National Park Service. *Promised Land on the Solomon: Black Settlement at Nicodemus, Kansas*. Washington, DC: U.S. Government Printing Office, 1986.
Yount, Lisa. *Blacks in the West*. New York: Facts On File, 1997.

Fort Verde

STATION OF BUFFALO SOLDIERS IN THE WEST
Camp Verde, Arizona

AT A GLANCE

Built: 1871–73

Military post established to protect the settlers of the Verde River valley

One of several sites throughout the West that were partially or completely garrisoned after the Civil War by black soldiers. This State Historic Park includes 10 acres with three of the original buildings still standing that once served as officers' quarters, as well as the administration building and part of the parade ground.

Address:

Fort Verde State Historic Park
P.O. Box 397
Camp Verde, AZ 86322
(520) 567-3275

> With the western migration of white settlers as well as African Americans, Native Americans began to see a steady invasion of their land. As members of the U.S. Armed Services, African Americans fought to defend settlements against those pushed out. From the Native Americans they received the name Buffalo Soldiers. From the U.S. government they received little.

In the midst of great dangers, the officers and men [of the 10th Cavalry] have maintained a gallant devotion to duty. . . . It cannot fail, sooner or later, to meet with due recognition.

—Colonel Benjamin H. Grierson,
commander of the 10th Cavalry

♦ ♦ ♦ ♦ ♦

Fort Verde today   (Courtesy of Fort Verde)

Military contributions made by African Americans form a vital part of U.S. history even though recognition of black soldiers' bravery in battle has been spotty. After resisting, George Washington finally admitted black soldiers into the Continental Army during the Revolutionary War, and 5,000 African Americans helped fight for American independence. And under pressure from black and white abolitionists, President Lincoln admitted black soldiers into the Union forces in 1863, two years into the Civil War. Black soldiers fought with great courage during both wars, as they have ever since—and their contribution is legendary. In Boston, for example, stands a monument to the 54th Regiment of Massachusetts Volunteer Infantry, the first black regiment to be recruited in the Northeast during the Civil War. On July 18, 1863, the 54th Regiment became famous for leading a staunch assault on Fort Wagner as part of the strategy to capture the Confederate city Charleston, South Carolina. Many members of the regiment were killed, including the white commanding officer Robert Gould Shaw. Sergeant William Carney of the 54th became the first African American to receive the Congressional Medal of Honor, for his bravery in protecting the American flag from Confederate capture. Members of the 54th are also notable for refusing to accept lower pay than their white counterparts for their 18 months of service—a stand that Congress finally recognized, increasing their pay retroactively.

Immediately after the end of the Civil War, large military cutbacks occurred, and most African Americans were discharged. But at the same time, with the western migration of white settlers as well as African Americans, Native Americans began to see a steady invasion of their land. The Cheyenne, Arapaho, Osage, Pawnee and other Plains tribes began to fight to hold on to their native homelands. As these battles flared into full-blown war, the U.S. Army increased its regiments. Military strength was needed on the western frontier. In 1866 African Americans were given full military status by Congress, and the army designated the 9th and 10th U.S. Cavalries as all-African-American regiments.

The 9th U.S. Cavalry, recruited from freed men in Louisiana and Kentucky, was first stationed in New Orleans among empty cotton presses and later served heroically in Texas against Comanche and Kiowa braves.

The 10th U.S. Cavalry was organized and headquartered at Fort Leavenworth in Kansas. There the first official African-American soldiers

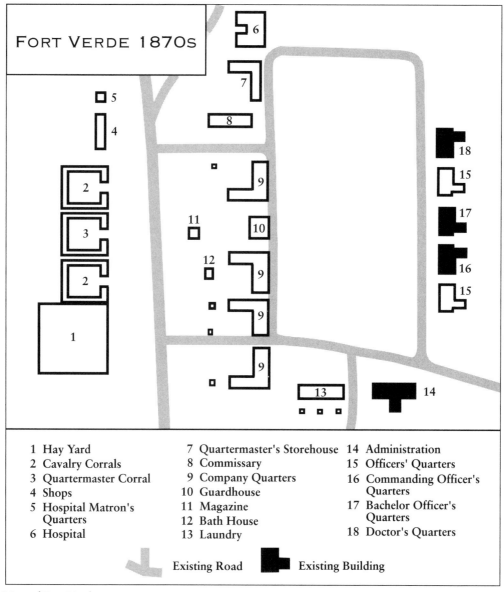

FORT VERDE 1870s

1 Hay Yard
2 Cavalry Corrals
3 Quartermaster Corral
4 Shops
5 Hospital Matron's Quarters
6 Hospital
7 Quartermaster's Storehouse
8 Commissary
9 Company Quarters
10 Guardhouse
11 Magazine
12 Bath House
13 Laundry
14 Administration
15 Officers' Quarters
16 Commanding Officer's Quarters
17 Bachelor Officer's Quarters
18 Doctor's Quarters

Existing Road   Existing Building

Map of Fort Verde

were given blue uniforms and equipment and immediately dispatched to posts scattered from Arizona to Texas, and from Wyoming to western Kansas.

The Cheyenne called them Buffalo Soldiers, no one is quite sure why— but it was clearly a term of respect, not insult. Members of the 10th Cavalry wore the name *Buffalo Soldier* with pride, making the buffalo image their military insignia.

These Buffalo Soldiers patrolled throughout the West, the length and breadth of Plains tribes' territories. They escorted wagon trains through ambush-laden territory. And they laid telegraph lines, built roads and forts and guarded railroad workers. They also fought in combat against Native Americans.

Although Fort Leavenworth, in Kansas, served as headquarters for the 10th U.S. Cavalry, prejudice excluded the Buffalo Soldiers from accommodation inside the fort. Instead they were forced to camp in the swampy surrounding area. (A 14-foot Buffalo Soldier Monument, dedicated by General Colin Powell on July 25, 1992, now stands in this area.)

From 1867 to 1869 Fort Larned, which is now a National Historic Site, was the first duty station for the 10th Cavalry men. Operating out of this Kansas fort, they assisted in guarding the famous Santa Fe Trail that ran south and west across Arizona and New Mexico.

At Fort Verde, the experience of I Troop of the 10th Cavalry was slightly better than at Fort Leavenworth. Stationed at this small Arizona fort from

Private William Johnston (on horseback at left), I Troop, 10th Cavalry, prepares to accompany a hunting party at Fort Verde, 1887. (Courtesy of Fort Verde)

FORT VERDE

Buffalo Soldiers with their mounts at Fort Verde (Courtesy of Fort Verde)

1886 to 1888, I Troop fully garrisoned the fort. Aside from white commanding officers, African-American soldiers had the place to themselves. Nonetheless, when they went into town, they ran into prejudice.

At Fort Verde, where several original buildings still stand, it's easy to imagine the Fort Verde of territorial Arizona, when I Troop, 10th Cavalry was there. The outer walls of these buildings were of *pice* construction. Pice is a technique for casting huge adobe (mud-brick) units using a temporary wooden form. Simpler and faster than making buildings of adobe bricks, this method made a stronger construction possible and was less susceptible to water damage.

Throughout the later years of the 1800s, the 9th and 10th U.S. Cavalries became the most-decorated regiments in U.S. Army history. These units had the lowest desertion rate of any unit in the army from 1867 to 1898, and 23 members received Congressional Medals of Honor for their courageous efforts and exceptional service under such harsh and rigid conditions.

Integration came to the armed services in 1952, and at that time the regiment was disbanded.

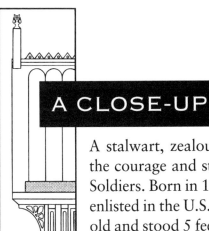

A CLOSE-UP

LINSAY KENDRICKS, 10TH CAVALRY

A stalwart, zealous soldier, Linsay Kendricks was typical of the courage and stamina displayed by the men called Buffalo Soldiers. Born in 1852 in Dry Ridge, Kentucky, Kendricks first enlisted in the U.S. Army on March 16, 1876. He was 24 years old and stood 5 feet 10¼ inches tall. Prior to joining the army, he had worked as a printer, horse tamer and cowboy.

Initially assigned to the Regimental Band of the 10th Cavalry, Kendricks gained a promotion in 1879 to sergeant when he was appointed regimental saddler, and without hesitation he reenlisted when his duty was up in 1881 at Fort Concho, Texas. Thereafter he served at Fort Davis with his regiment, followed by Fort Whipple in Arizona in 1885. At his own request, his rank was reduced to private so he could be assigned to a line company, serving in an area of combat. He was assigned to I Troop, 10th Cavalry on August 31, 1885, joining his outfit at Fort Verde in September 1885. Kendricks was promoted to corporal the following month.

Kendricks and I Troop, 10th Cavalry left Fort Verde on December 11, 1885 to participate in the campaign against the formidable Apache chief Geronimo. During this campaign Kendricks injured his back but did not report the injury because he did not want to miss action by being laid up in the hospital. I Troop, with Kendricks, was in the field between Fort Grant and Fort Thomas almost continuously in early 1886. Discharged at the end of his term, March 15, 1886 at Fort Verde, Kendricks had by this time qualified as a marksman. He reenlisted the following month.

In 1887 Kendricks suffered another back and kidney injury from a falling log that knocked him unconscious. Because the pain and bleeding subsided, he didn't go on sick report, but a doctor heard about the injury and assigned Kendricks to light duty for the remainder of his service. This was an order he ignored, joining a detail that was pushing a 6-mule team and wagon up the road near the San Carlos Indian Reservation. He injured himself again. The officer in charge of the detail picked him up and, reminding him of the light duty orders that he had ignored, relieved him. This time the injury led to an Honorable Discharge on a Surgeon's Certificate of Disability, on November 14, 1890.

Kendricks had saved $1,800 of his wages with which to start a new life. On discharge he was described as an honest, reliable man when entrusted with public property, as well as intelligent and "fairly sophisticated in his writing and composition." His army buddies remembered him as a powerful, strong man and a hearty eater. He continued to work outside the army in a wide variety of active jobs, even though he sustained various additional injuries. He died at age 75 in Indianapolis, Indiana.

The avid willingness of soldiers like Kendricks to meet danger and shoulder whatever work was at hand typified the Buffalo Soldiers, many of whom saw extensive action and laid their lives on the line for their country.

PRESERVING IT FOR THE FUTURE

Apache raids tapered off in the Fort Verde area by 1882, and the post became less important. In 1891 it was finally abandoned to the Department of the Interior, which sold it at public auction in 1899. Local citizens established a museum in the fort's former administration building in 1956 and donated several buildings to create Fort Verde State Historic Park in 1970. The site was placed on the National Register of Historic Places in 1971.

EXPLORING ♦ FURTHER

Readings on Buffalo Soldiers

Cox, Clinton. *The Forgotten Heroes: The Story of the Buffalo Soldiers.* New York: Scholastic, 1993.

Leckie. William H. *The Buffalo Soldiers: A Narrative of the Negro Cavalry in the West.* Norman: University of Oklahoma Press, 1967.

McGowan, Tom. *Lonely Eagles and Buffalo Soldiers: African Americans in World War II.* New York: Franklin Watts, 1995.

Reef, Catherine. *Buffalo Soldiers.* New York: Twenty-First Century Books, 1993.

Related Sites

Historical Museum at Fort Missoula
Building 322
Fort Missoula
Missoula, Montana 59801
(406) 728-3476

The 25th Infantry, stationed here from May 1888, had the unique distinction of testing bicycles for use by the military, making a 1,900-mile trip on bicycles from Fort Missoula to St. Louis.

Fort Larned National Historic Site
Rural Route 3
Larned, KS 67550
(316) 285-6911

Buffalo Soldiers stationed here served as escorts for wagon trains along the Santa Fe Trail. Park personnel give active demonstrations of living history on a number of topics, including Buffalo Soldier life. Nine restored sandstone buildings appear as they did in 1860.

Maggie Lena Walker Historic Site

HOME OF THE FIRST FEMALE BANK PRESIDENT
Richmond, Virginia

AT A GLANCE

Built: ca. 1883

Home of entrepreneur Maggie L. Walker, 1904–34

Located in the Jackson Ward Historical District, a 25-room, two-story, red-painted brick row house, Victorian Italianate style, with a Colonial Revival porch. Its structure and contents reflect the philosophy, taste and culture of its owner, Maggie Lena Walker. Originally nine rooms, the house was expanded during the time that the Walkers lived there and accommodated as many as 13 members of Maggie Walker's large extended family. The rooms contain many of the original items from the Walker period.

Address:

Maggie Walker House, 110 ¹/₂ East Leigh Street
Richmond, VA 22323, (804) 780-1380

Maggie Lena Walker founded the successful St. Luke Penny Savings Bank in 1903, becoming the first woman to establish and head an American bank. She used her stature to organize African-American women in her community in a series of strategies designed to foster black pride, as well as African-American economic, political and social presence in Richmond and throughout the country.

And the great all absorbing interest, this thing which has driven sleep from my eyes and fatigue from my body, is the love I bear women, our Negro women, hemmed, circumscribed with every imaginable obstacle in our way, blocked and held down by the fears and prejudices of the whites, ridiculed and sneered at by the intelligent blacks.

—Maggie Lena Walker, 1909

♦ ♦ ♦ ♦ ♦

When visitors first walk up to the trim, well-heeled Italianate town house at 110½ Leigh Street, primely located in the heart of the Richmond neighborhood called Jackson Ward, the house conveys a sense of pride, a consideration for tasteful surroundings and a flair for comfort. A tour of Maggie Lena Walker's house and a look at her life reveal all this, and much more. Fresh white trim sets off the bright red paint of the brick structure, and crisp green-and-white awnings shade the windows from the hot Virginia sun. Inside, every room reflects her intelligence, vivacity and energy. Maggie Lena Walker (ca. 1867–1934) was born black, female and poor in a society where prejudice made liabilities of all three. Somehow she seemed to transform even these liabilities into assets.

"I was not born with a silver spoon in my mouth, but with a laundry basket practically on my head," Walker was always quick to point out. Walker's mother was a former slave and cook's assistant who worked in the household of Elizabeth Van Lew, a famous spy for the Union who lived in Richmond, a city of the confederacy. Van Lew was single, eccentric and an ardent abolitionist, a kindly employer who encouraged education and opportunity among her employees. Maggie was born in Richmond, Virginia, on July 15, 1867 (or possibly two or three years earlier—there are no records), the daughter of Elizabeth Draper and Eccles Cuthbert, an Irish-born journalist who was for many years a correspondent for the *New York Herald*. Draper and Cuthbert were never married.

On May 27, 1868, Elizabeth Draper married William Mitchell, the butler in the Van Lew household. The Civil War was only recently over and Mitchell hoped to put slavery even farther behind him. Thinking that he could find

Maggie L. Walker's home (Courtesy of the National Park Service)

greater opportunities in the downtown job market, he moved his new family to a small clapboard house in downtown Richmond. There he found a position as a waiter at the nearby Saint Charles Hotel, the most elegant in town. Maggie's brother, John B., or Johnnie, was born in 1870.

But opportunity is not what came knocking six years later, when Maggie was about nine years old. Mitchell disappeared in February 1876, and an intensive five-day search finally led to the discovery of his body floating in the James River. Although the coroner pronounced William Mitchell's death a suicide, most people, including Mitchell's family, felt sure he had been murdered.

As a widow, Elizabeth Mitchell was faced with supporting a family of small children and raising them alone. She took in laundry, a way of making a living that enabled her to keep an eye on her children as she was working. While Maggie never had to drop out of school, she helped her mother—delivering and picking up laundry baskets to and from her mother's white clients, doing the shopping and taking care of her younger brother.

Maggie attended segregated Richmond schools for blacks in buildings that had no bathrooms. They did, however, have an excellent all-black faculty of teachers who numbered among the leaders of the community, and Maggie took advantage of everything they had to teach her.

During the Great Richmond Revival of the summer of 1878—a period when many religious meetings were held and many conversions took place—Maggie was baptized and joined the Sunday school at the First African Baptist Church, located around the corner from where she lived. She was 11 years old, and this group came to play a key part in her approach to life.

At the age of 14, she formed another important alliance by joining a black fraternity called the Independent Order of Saint Luke. Like many such societies that sprang up during these years, St. Luke provided an important well-spring of black pride and social bonds for its members—a sort of extended family—as well as some important economic advantages. Formed in Baltimore, Maryland, in 1867 just after the war, its original purpose was to form an insurance fund to provide for burials and to help the sick and wounded. The purpose mushroomed from there to offer broader insurance to its members, employment opportunities, and most important, an effective network of cooperative relationships. These organizations held a vital place in the life of the black community, and many African Americans considered them so important that they belonged to several.

At the time when Maggie Mitchell joined St. Luke in the 1880s, the organization of these societies was beginning to change from a strictly local structure to a central administration of many local councils. This centralization, coupled with membership drives and resulting increases in capital, began to place fraternal societies like St. Luke in an even stronger position for financing programs, making investments and establishing diversified businesses. Maggie joined the Chief of Good Idea Council #16 in Richmond. She soon ascended through the ritual positions and attended several conventions while still a student, gaining exposure to the possibilities St. Luke could offer its members.

For Maggie, a commitment to black equality and activism came early. As a student leader of the 1883 graduating class at all-black Armstrong Normal and High School, she and her classmates risked expulsion by objecting to separate black graduation exercises held in a church, while white students in Richmond received their diplomas in a local theater. Their school principal told them they could attend exercises in the theater, but they would have to sit in the balcony, a condition they refused to accept. Finally, as a compromise, Walker and her classmates agreed to receive diplomas in the school gymnasium. They hadn't obtained the integrated ceremony and equal recognition they had hoped for, but at least it wasn't "business as usual." It was one of Maggie's first experiences taking an aggressive position for racial equality.

After graduation, Maggie became a teacher—one of the few occupations open to educated black women. She taught elementary level classes for three years, with a starting salary of $35.00 a month. During these years she also took business training and worked as a collection agent, gaining experience in the business world.

Meanwhile, she had met a young man named Armstead Walker at an evening Sunday school meeting, and she married him on September 14, 1886. An 1875 normal school graduate, Walker worked at his father's prosperous bricklaying and construction business, later forming a partnership with his brother. He also served for 10 years as a mail carrier.

After her marriage Maggie Walker had to leave her teaching career, because married women were typically not accepted as teachers at that time. She did not, however, intend to stay behind the scenes, either in her marriage or her life, as indicated by her very modern statements concerning the nature of marriage:

> And since marriage is an equal partnership, I believe that the woman and the man are equal in power and should by consultation and agreement, mutually decide as to the conduct of the home and the government of the children.

With newfound time on her hands, she became even more active in the Independent Order of St. Luke, beginning with the 1895 convention, at which she submitted a resolution to establish a juvenile division. This division, as proposed by Walker, would contain Circles, formed by the local councils, and would be governed by female officers called Matrons. Her proposal was adopted by the convention, giving women a central and powerful position in the organization. Shortly thereafter Walker was elected Grand Matron, serving as chief of the new female officers, a position she retained for the rest of her life. The resulting St. Luke youth organization became an enormously effective vehicle for promoting black pride, savings, responsibility and mutual concern among African-American youths. Tens of thousands of children's lives were touched by it.

Walker's second big project was engineered outside the formal structure of St. Luke. A new company, the St. Luke Association, was formed by 25 Richmond councils of the Independent Order of St. Luke. The association's purpose was to purchase property for building St. Luke's headquarters, and Maggie Walker was secretary of the board. The association raised the money by holding bazaars and events and in 1903 completed a three-story hall.

By now Maggie Walker was a recognized leader, whose additional flair for the dramatic fit well with the organization's love of ritual and its trappings. St. Luke's, however, needed stronger central leadership. At the 1899 convention, Maggie Walker was chosen Right Worthy Grand Secretary. Inattention to cash flow had left the assets meager, and Walker took the position at half-salary to spare the organization's funds, which had dwindled to just $31.61. The former male secretary was skeptical that a woman could succeed at the job, but Maggie Walker went to work. She and her associates held membership drives extending into 22 states. Walker spoke wherever she could. In her low, persuasive voice, she talked about cooperative enterprise. She urged that the black community should be independent economically from the white community, that women should be independent from men. She called upon black women to enter the business world. She asked black consumers to shop at black businesses. Walker had a special message for women—she believed that the black community would never gain the strength it needed if women did not bring to the table their talent for cooperation and their considerable abilities. But she also believed that success would come only if women and men worked together. St. Luke was not a women's organization, and she encouraged men to participate, which they did. By 1924, the membership drives and other enterprises of St. Luke had resulted in a treasury containing $3,480,540.19. Walker continued as executive secretary for the rest of her life.

In 1902 Walker founded the *St. Luke Herald*, of which she became the editor—another position she held until the end of her life. The newspaper also became an important voice on the subjects of lynching, the position of black women and other political issues, and prominent blacks, including Booker T. Washington, numbered among its writers.

In 1903 Walker came to the conclusion that what the members of St. Luke needed was a bank of their own, an institution that would encourage thrift and economic gain and would, along with St. Luke itself, provide jobs for African Americans in the community. She spearheaded the foundation of the St. Luke Penny Savings Bank, of which she became president, serving in that capacity until 1931—the first female bank president in the country. The bank's slogan, in keeping with Maggie's philosophy that blacks should look out for their own interests was: "Bring It All Back Home."

When the Virginia Banking Division forced the separation of secret orders and their banks, the bank's name was changed to the Saint Luke Bank and Trust Company, and it soon became recognized as one of the best-managed and fastest-growing financial institutions in the world.

By 1904, when the Walkers bought the house at 110½ Leigh, Maggie Walker had risen to become a significant force in the black community of Richmond, and the stature of the house and the renovations she and her husband made reflected that position. When they bought the house, it had nine rooms. But by this time Maggie and Armstead's family had expanded. They had two sons, Russell Eccles Talmage Walker (born in 1890) and Melvin DeWitt Walker (born in 1897). A third, Armstead Mitchell Walker (born in 1893) died in infancy. Their household also included Maggie's mother, Elizabeth Mitchell; their adopted daughter, Margaret "Polly" Anderson; and after Polly's marriage, husband Maurice Payne, until his death in 1925. So in addition to adding central heating and electricity (somewhat innovative for the time), they also expanded the number of rooms.

Although she never lost her optimistic and determined outlook, Maggie Walker's life was haunted by tragedy. In addition to the loss of her father when she was nine and of a son before he had lived even a year, her brother Johnnie died an untimely death at age 23. An even greater blow came when, in a tragic accident in 1915, Russell mistook his father for a burglar, shooting and killing him. During the investigation that followed, Maggie stood by her son, but the loss was heartrending. Russell, too, died young, at the age of 33 in 1923.

Given these losses, Walker loved having her family around her, and her focus on family and an extended community is reflected in the way her house grew over the years. In 1922, the Walkers did extensive additional remodeling, adding rooms upstairs, a sitting room and laundry room downstairs, and remodeling the upstairs bathroom so that the two sons, now

Maggie Walker (right) and employees at the cashier's window at St. Luke's (Courtesy of the National Park Service)

grown, could live there with their families, as well as Polly Payne and her husband Maurice. Walker divided the second-floor bedroom area into family groupings, with rooms for the grandchildren near their parents' rooms.

Downstairs, the rooms are homey and comfortable. The kitchen served as a family gathering place, and here Polly, who was an excellent cook, prepared all the meals. It was a good place to talk, and the poets Langston Hughes and Countee Cullen and educator Mary McLeod Bethune all relaxed here with Maggie Walker. The sitting room provided an area where Melvin and Russell could relax with their friends, or sometimes conduct business meetings. Here too, Melvin often listened to music on the Victrola. Both sons worked for St. Luke—Russell, who had studied accounting and life insurance, worked for the Order's insurance division, while Melvin served as a cashier at the St. Luke Penny Savings Bank.

Maggie Walker loved to entertain, and the dining room and parlors were appointed to welcome the many public figures that she knew. Walker's granddaughters recalled the family also using the dining room " . . . on weekends when she'd have the big Sunday dinners (all of us together) around the table . . ." At Christmas time, a big tree was placed in the bay window of the front parlor, or sometimes in the library, and Walker occasionally held meetings here. This was the room for big events, as well, such as wakes or weddings.

In 1905 St. Luke embarked on one more all-black enterprise, a retail department store called the Emporium. Supremely designed to "bring it all back home," this black-owned enterprise provided substantial employment for African-American women, both on its board of directors and in the store. Located in a three-story building on Broad Street, Richmond's main artery, the Emporium encouraged members of the Richmond African-American community to buy black. Now St. Luke was clearly attempting to cut a piece of the retail trade pie that had always belonged to white businesses, and white retailers fought back with overt pressure. Black consumers' preference for the labels carried by the white stores also took a bite out of profits and in the end the Emporium lost money and was forced to close in 1911.

Maggie Walker (third from left, seated), 1917   (Courtesy of the National Park Service)

In 1907, Walker fell on the front steps of her home, breaking her knee cap and causing irreparable damage to nerves and tendons. The excruciating pain she experienced as a result caused her to cut back her activities to some degree. As time went on the condition grew progressively worse and complications set in. From 1928 on, she used a wheelchair to get around, but the inconvenience scarcely slowed her down. In the parlor, visitors can still see a wheelchair very similar to the wicker-and-wood chair she used every day. In 1928 Walker also added an elevator at the back of the house so that she could continue to use the upstairs of the house, and she had her Packard remodeled so that she could roll her wheelchair right into the car—both of which visitors can view. Upstairs, too, she made changes to make life in a wheelchair pleasanter, enclosing a sunporch at the front of the house from which she could survey the entire neighborhood. She also added a kitchenette off her bedroom, where Polly sometimes came to prepare meals for Maggie, and which other members of the family also used for convenience.

Maggie Walker was senior partner in two mergers that resulted in 1931 in the formation of the Consolidated Bank and Trust Company, which still exists today, located diagonally across the street from the original St. Luke Penny Savings Bank, on First and Clay Streets in downtown Richmond. She became chairman of the board of this institution, and under the name Consolidated Bank and Trust Company, Walker's original institution survives today. Its makeup only slightly changed by the mergers, Consolidated Bank and Trust claims the distinction, due to this lineage from the St. Luke Penny Savings Bank, of being the oldest continually black-operated bank in the United States.

Walker took a leadership role in the local chapter of the National Association for the Advancement of Colored People (NAACP, formed locally in 1917) and was also a national leader in the NAACP, serving as a board member from 1928 to 1934. Throughout her life she was active in many organizations, including the National Association of Colored Women and the Virginia Industrial School for Girls. She organized and served as president of the St. Luke Educational Fund, which helped black children get an education, and during her lifetime she was appointed by several Virginia governors to numerous posts, in which she served with distinction.

Maggie Lena Walker died of diabetic gangrene on December 15, 1934. The memorial services held at First American Baptist Church had the largest attendance in the history of Richmond.

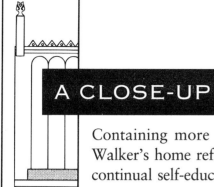

A CLOSE-UP | MAGGIE WALKER'S LIBRARY

Containing more than 1,000 books, the library in Maggie Walker's home reflects, not only her active mind and belief in continual self-education, but also evokes much of her philosophy about black pride. The walls are covered with photographs of family, key figures in the life of St. Luke, and other black leaders of varying viewpoints, including W. E. B. DuBois, Booker T. Washington, Mary McLeod Bethune and Mary Church Terrell. They were all people she knew personally. Washington often wrote for the *St. Luke Herald* and gave a speech in Richmond at Walker's invitation. DuBois was a fellow member of the national board of the NAACP. And Bethune and Terrell were

The library   (Courtesy of the National Park Service)

MAGGIE LENA WALKER HISTORIC SITE

fellow members of the National Association of Colored Women. In a speech given by Walker in 1909, she questioned how blacks could have pride in themselves if "... in their homes were the books, pictures, photographs, and busts of another race." Her own home reflected that philosophy.

The room's shelves are filled with a wide range of books, many of them by or about blacks. There are also popular novels, works of Mark Twain and Shakespeare; books on accounting, business, and finance; and Latin and Greek classics.

Walker also displayed the family's numerous diplomas on the walls, including hers, Armstead's, her sons', and an honorary master of science degree awarded to her in 1925 by Virginia Union University for her work in business.

Above all, Maggie Walker's library is a comfortable room, cool in summer, where members of the family came to read or meet—clearly a room that was meant to be used and was.

PRESERVING IT FOR THE FUTURE

After Maggie Lena Walker's death in 1934, Hattie Walker, her daughter-in-law, owned the house until she died in 1974. Her daughter, Maggie Laura Walker, inherited the house and sold it to the government in 1979. The Maggie L. Walker Historical Foundation, formed in 1974, had informed the family that they were interested in the house as a historical museum, and the National Park Service and the foundation formed a working agreement. The Maggie L. Walker National Historic Site was established by Congress in 1978, and restoration to the house's 1927 appearance is ongoing.

EXPLORING ♦ FURTHER

Readings by Maggie Walker

Walker, Maggie. *Addresses—Maggie Walker*. Richmond, VA: Maggie Walker National Historic Site, 1909, 1921, 1931.

———. *Diaries of Maggie Walker*. Richmond, VA: Maggie Walker National Historic Site, 1921, 1931.

Readings about Maggie Walker

Bird, Caroline. "The Innovators: Maggie Walker, Kate Gleason." *Enterprising Women*. New York: Norton, 1976.

Brown, Elsa Barkley. "Womanist Consciousness: Maggie Lena Walker and the Independent Order of Saint Luke," *Signs: Journal of Women in Culture and Society*. Vol. 14, No. 3, 1989.

———. "Maggie Lena Walker," *Encyclopedia of Southern Culture*. Edited by Charles Wilson and William Ferris. Chapel Hill: University of North Carolina Press, 1989.

Duckworth, Margaret. "Maggie Walker, Bank President," *Epic Lives: One Hundred Black Women Who Made a Difference*. Edited by Jessie Carney Smith. Detroit, MI: Visible Ink Press, 1993.

Field, Sue, and Stephanie Halloran. "Maggie Walker—Lifting as We Climb." Richmond, VA: Maggie Walker Papers, Maggie Walker National Historic Site, January 1976.

Jordan, Daniel. "Indomitable Maggie Walker." *Commonwealth* 48 (March 1981): 32–4.

Related Places—Other Early Entrepreneurs

Madame C. J. Walker Home

Born Sarah Breedlove, C. J. Walker married at 14 to escape an abusive family life, but it is said that her husband was killed by a lynch mob when she was only 20. After just scraping by for years at a poverty level, she invented a hair preparation for straightening black women's hair more easily and safely than the methods then in use. By steadily building her business with new products and wider distribution, by 1914 her company grossed earnings over $1 million. More important, she used herself as a promotion for the idea of black economic self-help. Lewaro, the mansion she bought on the Hudson River, still stands, with a plaque commemorating Walker's achievements, although the house is not open to the public.

Mary McLeod Bethune Home

HOME OF AN EDUCATOR AND ACTIVIST
Daytona Beach, Florida

AT A GLANCE

Built: ca. 1914

Home of educator and activist Mary McLeod Bethune, 1923–55

A spacious but unpretentious two-story, white clapboard house with a big front porch and nine rooms, situated on the campus of the school that she founded in 1904.

Address:

Mary McLeod Bethune Foundation
640 Second Avenue
Daytona Beach, FL 32114
(904) 255-1401

> Born to former slaves, by the end of Mary McLeod Bethune's lifetime, she had founded a college, served as an adviser to five U.S. presidents and had received the Haitian Medal of Honor for her work in the cause of human rights and education.

You can never leave me behind.

—Mary McLeod Bethune

◆ ◆ ◆ ◆

Mary McLeod Bethune's home   (Courtesy of Bethune-Cookman College)

Charismatic, direct and humanitarian, Mary McLeod Bethune was also a powerful and unstoppable force in the cause of racial equality. She deftly made use of her shrewd understanding of politics, combined with her straightforward manner and frankly engaging personality, to raise funds, persuade presidents and, if necessary, move mountains. Visitors to her house can see photo after photo of groups in which Bethune is always in the center of the front row. Even an innocuous photo-taking session was to her an opportunity to make a point. When asked why she was always up front and center, she would quip, "Because you can never leave me behind."

But visitors to the Mary McLeod Bethune Foundation, the home where she lived for more than 30 years of her life, also find another side to Bethune, as well. She was a collector of knickknacks and treasures; she surrounded herself with photographs of family, and with gifts and remembrances of friends both powerful and downtrodden, educated and unlettered, wealthy and penniless. Her niece and housekeeper, Georgia McLeod, ritualistically laid out her nightclothes on the bed each morning, her slippers on the footstool nearby, ready for Bethune to retire whenever she was ready. You can see them still, laid out as Georgia placed them the day Bethune died. On the bedroom door, you can see Bethune's favorite dress, an elegant black embroidered gown that she always wore to occasions of state, concerts and special events. Proud of her achievements, too, with the dress she always wore a medallion, the Haitian Medal of Honor, given to her by the government of Haiti in honor of her work in the cause of education and human equality. A huge dresser mirror on one wall of the room reflects the tall, stately headboard of her bed and the deep rose walls and maroon carpet, now well worn with time. The furniture is comfortable and well used, a rocking chair and a marble-topped bureau and table. This was Mary McLeod Bethune's inner sanctum. Always aware of the roots she came from, she kept a picture of the log cabin in which she was born and a portrait of her parents on the wall by her bedside.

When Mary McLeod was born in 1875 near Mayesville, South Carolina, no one in her family had ever been given a chance to learn to read or write. She was the 15th of 17 children of former slaves Samuel and Patsy McLeod, and she was the first born free to her parents, who were by then sharecropping on a plot of land they had been lucky enough to acquire. When a

Mary McLeod Bethune's bedroom. Note the nightclothes laid out for her and her favorite dress hanging on the door. (Courtesy of Bethune-Cookman College)

Presbyterian missionary stopped by their home one day in 1884, she volunteered to take one of the McLeods' children to Trinity Presbyterian Mission School to learn to read and write. Pick the most eager and brightest, the one most likely to benefit, she told Mary's parents, and out of all 17 they picked Mary, because she was different, her mother said—homely, but very bright. She was nine years old, and she trudged daily the 4 or 5 miles on country roads to and from school.

It was the beginning of a long career in which education and its importance played a key part. Obtaining a scholarship, Mary McLeod went on to attend the Scotia Seminary in Concord, North Carolina, for six years. There her training centered on religious principles, combined with development of "culture and refinement" and vocational skills—mostly housekeeping skills. She saw this period as preparation for mission work. But when she applied for a position as a missionary to Africa, she was told that African Americans could not be chosen for this work. Her disappointment was intense, and she later admitted it was the greatest disappointment of her life.

But Mary McLeod was never a quitter, always turning to whatever avenues were open to her and pursuing them with courage and conviction. In this case, the only avenue at the time for a woman of her education and color was teaching. So beginning in 1893, she pursued further studies at the all-white Moody Bible Institute in Chicago, afterward obtaining a position teaching at the Haines Institute in Augusta, Georgia, in 1895.

Three years later she married a tall, handsome man named Albertus Bethune, settling in Savannah where he found work as a porter. Mary gave birth to their son, Albert. The Bethunes lived together for about eight years, after which they separated. Even though they remained legally married until the death of Albertus in 1918, theirs was not a happy marriage and domestic social structures never played an important part in Mary McLeod Bethune's life or philosophy.

In the meantime she continued the career she had begun, teaching in Presbyterian schools from 1900 to 1904 in Sumter, Georgia, and Palatka, Florida.

By 1904 a 29-year-old woman with a child and only $1.50 in starting capital, Mary McLeod Bethune founded the Daytona Educational and Industrial Institute for Girls in Florida. Classes began with five little girls as students, using dry goods boxes as benches in a rented house. It was the first school in Florida founded by and for blacks to offer an education beyond the elementary level. In the beginning the school had only one room and five students, but it grew rapidly. Within two years Bethune had attracted 250 students to her school, and she had also founded the Tomoka Missions and in 1911 the McLeod Hospital. She had begun to make her mark, receiving national attention for her work. Like Booker T. Washington, she had a great talent for fund-raising, and within a short time, she began to secure sizable donations from wealthy contributors, many of them white. John D. Rockefeller, for example, became one of the school's early supporters—both monetarily and psychologically—after hearing a performance by its choir. And visitors to Bethune's house today can still see the china cabinet and set of crystal in Bethune's dining room given to her by Rockefeller.

Bethune's school ultimately became Bethune-Cookman College, having merged in 1923 with Cookman Institute, a Methodist school for black males opened in 1872. That same year Bethune moved into the house on

Second Avenue in Daytona Beach. By 1941 the school had become a four-year liberal arts institution, with a career-oriented curriculum and a coeducational, residential campus. Since 1960 the college has received continuous accreditation from the Southern Association of Colleges and Schools.

Bethune approached education for young black women in her day with much the same precepts that Booker T. Washington used for young black men. Her objective was to build opportunity for African-American girls, and she encouraged a philosophy based on Christian principles and the basic human consideration involved in good manners. To that formula she added development of domestic skills and teacher training. It was a place to begin. Bethune believed that labor and accomplishment could increase self-esteem and that education could enable African Americans to achieve all-important economic independence. Slavery had robbed them of that power in the past; now, with freedom and education, she felt all that could be changed. A tireless fighter for equality, Bethune could hold her ground, but she spoke out for universal love, rather than militancy. Partly because of this, she succeeded in getting white people to listen who had never listened before, and who might have been put off by more aggressive and radical tones.

Mary McLeod Bethune was not naive. She knew that change came about through power, and she could see that she could gain access to power through her nonthreatening position as a woman. She reinforced that nonthreatening voice of reason with good manners and a belief in domestic virtues. Bethune recognized that political power was in the hands of white politicians, and she found ways to press her advantage with them. Once she gained national influence, she also knew how to translate that strength into influence in her own community. She steadily developed avenues of influence and used them knowledgeably and skillfully to advance black progress.

She was an adviser in the administrations of Calvin Coolidge, Herbert Hoover, Franklin Delano Roosevelt, Harry S. Truman and Dwight D. Eisenhower. Thanks to the national recognition that Bethune received for her work at the college, President Herbert Hoover asked Bethune to serve as a member of Hoover's Committee for Child Welfare.

Her greatest contribution came, however, during the administration of Franklin Delano Roosevelt. When FDR was elected president of the United

States in 1932, however, the African-American population had no reason to expect any good to come their way in the New Deal he proposed. First of all he was a Democrat, and many blacks still remembered the Democratic Party as the southern party opposed to emancipation and the supporter of states' rights legislation that had set back the clock on hoped for advances in racial equality. Moreover, FDR's track record on racial issues was poor: he had courted the antiblack southern politicians in order to gain office, and once in office, he would have to get along with them in order to get anything done. For these reasons more than two-thirds of voting African-Americans cast their ballot against FDR in the 1932 election. With hard times at the top of the president's agenda, there was little hope that he would address the controversial issue of the plight of the black population.

To a large degree the black population was right, especially in the beginning. Most of the New Deal programs were not designed fairly, and blacks benefiting from the programs of the National Recovery Administration (NRA), the Civilian Conservation Corps (CCC) and others were, not only far outnumbered by whites, but regularly received significantly less. But by 1934, things began to change. Vocal protests began to be heard, and the number of registered African-American voters climbed to numbers that could no longer be ignored. Pressure was building up from disparate groups. The radical Left and the labor movement, intellectuals and southern liberals, all for their own reasons, began to campaign for racial equality, and specifically, for racial reforms in the New Deal. Now FDR had to pay attention, while trying to mollify those who wanted to retain the status quo.

He appointed Mary McLeod Bethune his adviser on minority affairs, making her the highest ranking black woman in the New Deal administration. In this capacity, Bethune met frequently with President Roosevelt—six or seven times a year—and the White House doors were always open to her. Over time Roosevelt became more egalitarian. He invited African Americans to the White House, spoke before black organizations, associated himself with anti-lynching campaigns and anti-poll tax legislation. He listened to Bethune when she had requests, and she pushed steadily—both in public and in private—for greater sensitivity in New Deal programs to issues of race. She also gained considerable credibility in the black community as a champion of black causes and as the leader of an informal

Mary McLeod Bethune   (Courtesy of Bethune-Cookman College)

group of black federal officials that became known as the Black Cabinet. The causes that she put her influence behind included anti-lynching activities, the so-called Scottsboro boys (a group of young men in Alabama who were convicted and sentenced to death on negli gible evidence) and rights for black sharecroppers.

The Black Cabinet, or Black Brain Trust, as the press dubbed this group, was composed of black men and women appointed to administrative positions by FDR (he appointed a significantly larger number than had any of his predecessors). They formed a group that they called the Federal Council on Negro Affairs, although it had no official capacity, and they met periodically—often in Bethune's Washington home. The president had—probably intentionally—appointed none of the black officials in his administration to positions high enough for implementation of policy, but through their presence, especially as a bloc, they succeeded in having an effect. In the words of one historian, "They made white New Dealers marginally more sensitive to the needs of blacks; and they made the federal government seem more comprehensible and relevant to blacks."

When the National Youth Administration (NYA) was founded in 1935, FDR chose Mary McLeod Bethune as director of the Division of Negro

Affairs, a position she accepted in 1936 and held until 1943. The purpose of the NYA was to marshal efforts in all the agencies to increase opportunities for youth—providing jobs for college students that otherwise would have to drop out for lack of funds and offering on-the-job training for out-of-work youths who had left school. In this post Bethune was in a position to promote one of her prime causes: jobs and job training for youth and women. Bethune pressed for real training opportunities—not just park clean-up and janitorial jobs that, once completed, left the employees scarcely better off than when they had started.

In 1935 Bethune also founded the National Council of Negro Women and served as its president until 1949. Still vital and active today, this organization became strongly influential in the African-American community, publishing the *Aframerican Woman's Journal*, which advocated "that Negro History be taught in the public schools of the country." Bethune also became director of the National Business League, the National Urban League, and the Commission on Interracial Cooperation, as well as vice president of the National Association for the Advancement of Colored People (NAACP).

During these years, Bethune took on a racial adviser at-large capacity within the administration, which greatly broadened her influence. Although no appointment was ever made, her input was welcomed and taken very seriously. In addition to her frequent personal meetings with FDR, she also developed a strong friendship with his wife, Eleanor, who was enormously influential within the administration. Bethune advised on a wide range of issues involving racial sensitivity. When auto entrepreneur Henry Ford planned to break a strike using nonunion African Americans, through a long memo to Eleanor Roosevelt, Bethune warned FDR of the dire impact of this move on the African-American community. When federal housing in Detroit intended for black families was going to be allotted instead to white families, she pointed out the outrage that this plan would cause. Many changes originating with Bethune took place after a meeting between Bethune and Eleanor Roosevelt. From Bethune, Eleanor gained an increased sensitivity to and understanding of the country's racial problems, and Bethune relied on Eleanor to press for safeguarding black voting rights, the abolition of the poll tax (which discriminated against the poor, including blacks) and an anti-lynching law.

As the NAACP summed up the progress of the time, "It is true that the millennium in race relations did not arrive under Roosevelt. But cynics and scoffers to the contrary, the great body of Negro citizens made progress."

If that is true, it is in large measure due to the efforts of Mary McLeod Bethune. Bethune's legacy is enormous. Before Bethune, black women were invisible both politically and socially. Thanks to her leadership, black women today have become a sustained influence for social change and a steady and consistent presence in politics and the business world.

In 1935 Bethune received the Spingarn Award, the Frances A. Drexel Award in 1936 and the Thomas Jefferson Medal in 1942, and honors continued to pour in. On May 18, 1955, her niece Georgia McLeod found Mary McLeod Bethune on the porch at her home in Daytona Beach, where she had lived for 32 years. A heart attack had stopped her short in the midst of her morning routine in her house, surrounded by the school she had founded. The school and house remain there still, monuments to her considerable contributions to black education and the improvement of race relations.

A CLOSE-UP | FRIENDSHIP AND STAINED GLASS

In the office on the first floor of Mary McLeod Bethune's home, behind her desk, a colorful stained-glass window filters the light pouring in from the hot Florida sun. It was a gift given to her by Albert and Jesse Danielson, a wealthy white couple who one night found themselves hopelessly lost in the black section of Daytona Beach. Regular winter visitors to southern Florida, they were, however, unaccustomed to driving, and, without their usual chauffeur, hadn't the faintest idea how to get where they wanted to go. They were completely lost. Coming as they did

Bethune's office on the first floor of her home   (Courtesy of Bethune-Cookman College)

from an isolated and sheltered existence, they had never even met an African American before, and they had no idea what to expect. Frightened, bewildered and confused, they no longer knew which way to turn, when Bethune found them, huddled shivering in their car. Gently, she coaxed them out and convinced them that they should come home with her. Then she insisted that they should stay with her until she could help them find their way the next day.

Bethune's generosity, kindness and command of the situation impressed the couple, but as they talked, they noticed something that impressed them even more: a great wisdom and depth of character. The Danielsons long looked back on this experience as a high point in their lives.

Years later, when they sold their estate, they dismantled the stained-glass windows they had on their property and shipped them to those who had influenced them most greatly. In memory of that night when Mary McLeod Bethune opened her home to total strangers, they sent her one of the stained-glass windows for her office.

PRESERVING IT FOR THE FUTURE

Built in about 1914 the house became Bethune's home in 1923. In 1953 she opened the house to the public, while she was still living there, and visitors touring through often came across her calmly working at her desk. After Bethune's death the house was closed for a time. Georgia McLeod continued to live there for several years, and Bethune's foster son Edward Rodriguez became the curator. Rodriguez died in 1992. As indicated by a marker in front of the building, the National Park Service of the U.S. Department of the Interior designated the Mary McLeod Bethune Foundation a National Historic Landmark in 1975. On Bethune's 102nd birthday, July 10, 1977, a second marker was erected by the Association for the Study of Afro-American Life and History in cooperation with the Amoco Foundation. Thousands of visitors tour the home each year.

EXPLORING ◆ FURTHER

Readings by and about Mary McLeod Bethune

Bethune, Mary McLeod. "My Secret Talks with FDR," *The Negro in Depression and War: Prelude to Revolution 1930–1945.* Edited by Bernard Sternsher. Chicago: Quadrangle Books, 1969.

Holt, Rackham. *Mary McLeod Bethune.* Garden City, NY: Doubleday, 1964.

McKissack, Patricia, and Frederick McKissack. *Mary McLeod Bethune.* Chicago, Children's Press, 1992.

Ross, B. Joyce. "Mary McLeod Bethune and the National Youth Administration: A Case Study of Power Relationships in the Black Cabinet of Franklin D. Roosevelt," *Journal of Negro History.* 60 (January 1975):1–28.

Sitkoff, Harvard. *A New Deal for Blacks.* New York: Oxford University Press, 1978.

Smith, Elaine. "Mary McLeod Bethune." *Notable American Women: The Modern Period.* Vol. I. Cambridge, MA: Harvard University Press, 1980.

———. "Mary McLeod Bethune, Government Official, Activist," *Epic Lives: One Hundred Black Women Who Made a Difference.* Edited by Jessie Carney Smith. Detroit, MI: Visible Ink Press, 1993.

Other Places of Interest

Mary McLeod Bethune Birthplace Historical Marker
U.S. 76 at Lafayette Street
Mayesville, SC 29104
(800) 688-4748

Historical marker marks the birthplace of Mary McLeod Bethune.

Bethune Museum and Archives
1318 Vermont Avenue
Washington, DC 20005
(202) 332-1233; (202) 332-9201

Formerly Bethune's home in Washington, D.C., where she lived during her years working on New Deal projects; now houses a museum and archives, the largest repository of information on black women and their organizations, including standing exhibits on the career of Mary McLeod Bethune and on the commitment of black women to social change.

Statue of Mary McLeod Bethune
Lincoln Park
East Capitol Street
East of the Capitol, between 11th and 13th Streets
Washington, DC 20002

Statue by Robert Berks of Bethune with two children; she holds a walking stick that belonged to President Franklin Delano Roosevelt, given to Bethune by Eleanor Roosevelt after FDR's death. Erected in 1974, it is the first monument to an African American ever raised in Washington, D.C.

Martin Luther King, Jr., National Historic Site

HOME OF A HUMAN RIGHTS CHAMPION
Atlanta, Georgia

AT A GLANCE

Built: 1895

Birthplace and childhood home of Martin Luther King, Jr., 1929–44

A park of 52.3 acres that includes the birthplace of Martin Luther King, Jr.; Ebenezer Baptist Church, where he, his father and grandfather preached; King's tomb; the community where he grew up; and several other sites of interest have been designated part of the Martin Luther King, Jr., National Historic Site. The Martin Luther King, Jr., Center for Nonviolent Social Change is also located inside park boundaries.

Address:
The Martin Luther King, Jr., National Historic Site
526 Auburn Avenue, NE
Atlanta, GA 28802
(404) 331-3920

Here, within this neighborhood surrounding Auburn Avenue in Atlanta, world-renowned civil rights leader and Nobel Peace Prize recipient Martin Luther King, Jr., was born, grew up, preached, worshipped and is buried.

. . . when the history books are written in the future, somebody will have to say, "There lived a race of people, black people . . . who had the moral courage to stand up for their rights."

—Martin Luther King, Jr., Montgomery bus boycott

♦ ♦ ♦ ♦ ♦

Martin Luther King, Jr.,'s birthplace (Courtesy of Atlanta Convention and Visitors Bureau, © Kevin C. Rose)

Martin Luther King, Jr. (1929-64), was above all a conciliatory revolutionary. Throughout his life he battled constantly to end racism and economic oppression, but at the same time he worked to achieve social reconciliation. He led marches, sit-down strikes and face-to-face confrontations. He challenged the status quo and provoked change. He spoke passionately to huge gatherings and led them in his theme song "We Shall Overcome." He spent time in jail. Yet he wanted peace between the races. His two-pronged approach to change through confrontation and conciliation was both his greatest gift and his greatest flaw.

When Martin Luther King, Jr., was born on January 15, 1929 in his maternal grandfather's home on Auburn Avenue, he was born into a family deeply imbued in the social consciousness of a Christian doctrine. Both his father and grandfather were Baptist ministers at nearby Ebenezer Baptist Church, and both used their pulpits to preach social and political activism. His grandfather Adam Daniel ("A. D.") Williams had helped found the Atlanta Chapter of the National Association for the Advancement of Colored People (NAACP).

The time and place no doubt also influenced King. What is now called Sweet Auburn Historic District was home to King as he was growing up and was the soul and pride of black Atlanta from the 1890s to the mid-1900s. A business, residential and entertainment enclave along Auburn Avenue east of Five Points, this small section of town is often referred to as black Atlanta's main artery. It has produced men and women who influenced the history of the city, state and nation. This area encouraged a belief in success and provided an illustration to young Martin that African Americans could achieve economic success despite the limited opportunities caused by the handicap of legal segregation.

In this neighborhood a thriving business class began to emerge, represented by churches, banks, insurance companies, doctors' and dentists' offices, beauty parlors and funeral homes. A business college and newspaper had been established. Sweet Auburn breathed success and possibilities.

Built in 1895, the Queen Anne–style, nine-room, two-story house at 501 Auburn was purchased in 1909 for $3,500 by A. D. Williams. He and his wife, Jenny Parks Williams, raised their family there, and 17 years later, on Thanksgiving Day 1926, an energetic young man who would become known as Martin Luther King, Sr., married their daughter Alberta

Williams. He and his bride moved into a room upstairs, and in this house their three children were born, Christine (1927), Martin Luther, Jr., (1929) and Alfred Daniel Williams (1930).

Young M. L., as he was called, grew up playing baseball, football and basketball, and occasionally, with his brother, getting chased off the play equipment at the nearby school yard of the Lady of Lourdes Catholic school. He didn't like practicing the piano, although he took lessons, but he did enjoy trips to the public library and soon began building a library of his own. He, his sister and brother had regular chores around the house, which was nestled among other, similar turn-of-the-century, gable-roofed frame homes. His grandfather Williams was an influential preacher-activist. Young Martin's father took over the pastorate at the Ebenezer Church after Williams's death in 1931, where he, too, spoke out strongly on activist issues. But, while the Kings lived comfortably, their house wasn't extravagantly furnished. A plain though handsome wood mantel with marble inset graced the parlor, which contained attractive overstuffed

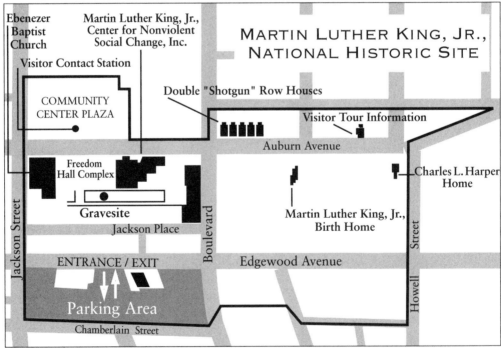

Map of the Martin Luther King, Jr., National Historic Site and surrounding historic district

Victorian furniture—protected by crocheted doilies in the fashion of the time—and, of course, the piano, which Martin's mother played with an innate musicality and an enthusiasm not shared by her older son. The family continued to live at the home on 501 Auburn until 1941, when Martin was 12, and they moved to a nearby brick house. Today, 501 Auburn, NE, is known as the Martin Luther King, Jr., Birth Home—a National Historic Landmark since 1977. The National Park Service began managing the site in 1980.

Following in the professional footsteps of his father and grandfather before him, Martin Luther King, Jr., graduated from Morehouse College, an all-black school in Atlanta, in 1948, obtaining his bachelor of divinity (BD) degree three years later from Crozer Theological Seminary in Chester, Pennsylvania. From there he went on to Boston University on a scholarship to earn his Ph.D. in systematic theology in 1955.

King first gained national prominence through his moral and political leadership during the Montgomery, Alabama bus boycott in 1955 to 1956. King was minister of the Dexter Avenue Baptist Church in Montgomery when, on December 1, 1955, a slender black seamstress named Rosa Parks was arrested for refusing to give up her seat on a Montgomery bus to a white man.

For years in Montgomery, and in most southern towns and cities, African Americans had had to put up with the indignities of "separate but equal" facilities of nearly every kind. Taxicab stands, schools, public restrooms and drinking fountains were only available to blacks if they were labeled "colored only." Moreover, the black facilities were never equal. Black residential areas had become ghettos, and African Americans could not live anywhere else. The bus system in Montgomery required black passengers to pay at the front of the bus and then get off and walk around to the rear of the bus, where they re-entered to sit in the back—the only area where they were allowed to ride. White bus drivers would often drive away before a paid passenger could even make it to the rear door. Additionally, when the bus was full, if a white passenger needed a seat, any black passenger was required to yield to the white passenger.

Though gallingly unjust, the system was law. Rosa Parks made headlines all over the nation when she was arrested in Montgomery, and her action began a bus boycott by the entire black community, led by Martin Luther King, Jr.

After her arrest, Rosa Parks lost her job as a seamstress in a department store. Her husband, a barber, was told not to discuss the boycott or mention Rosa's name to customers, and he left his job, too, stating that he would not work in a shop where his wife's name was unwelcome.

The bus boycott was in many ways harder on the boycotters than on the income of the Montgomery transit lines. Boycotters still needed to get to work, to doctors, to stores and post offices. But now they had no way to get there. Churches set up substitute taxi and bus services, and individuals volunteered the use of their cars. Many people walked places they would otherwise have taken the bus. It took a full year to win the point, but the boycotters, under King's leadership, did not give up. Even though King's house was bombed in January 1956, he continued to lead the boycott, emulating the passive-resistance techniques used so successfully by Mohandas Gandhi against the British ruling class in India. Ultimately, the bus boycott led to integration of Montgomery city buses. In November 1956 the U.S. Supreme Court ruled that Jim Crow laws, such as the one Rosa Parks violated in Montgomery, were unconstitutional.

This success encouraged others to demonstrate for their rights across the South. The Southern Christian Leadership Conference (SCLC) formed in Atlanta in 1957 to coordinate civil rights efforts, and Martin Luther King was elected president. In 1960 a group of black students who were denied service at a Greensboro, North Carolina lunch counter staged the first sit-in for civil rights. The civil rights movement had begun. New organizations sprang up to fight for the cause. That same year the Student Non-Violent Coordinating Committee (SNCC) formed, counting among its members Julian Bond, Stokely Carmichael, H. Rap Brown and John Lewis. In contrast to King and the SCLC, this was a younger, more secular group.

In 1959 King became copastor with his father of the Ebenezer Baptist Church in Atlanta, now located within the historic district. But the high profile King gained as civil rights activist continually placed him, not only in a position of influence, but also in danger. While signing autographs in Harlem for his book *Stride Toward Freedom* (1958) a mentally unstable black woman walked up and stabbed him. Though the injury was not severe, a less courageous man might have toned down his activities. King pressed on.

In 1960 King urged lunch counter sit-ins throughout the South, encouraged "freedom riders" to break segregation laws on interstate buses in 1961 and in 1963 he plunged into a major antisegregation campaign in Birmingham, Alabama. In Birmingham he met with stiff opposition from police chief Eugene "Bull" Connor, who used police dogs and water from high-pressure fire hoses to dispel the demonstrations. King was arrested and spent eight days in jail, during which time he wrote his famous *Letter from a Birmingham Jail*, in which he admonished white liberals for being faint-hearted and counseling him to back off.

August 28, 1963 saw 250,000 African Americans marching through the summer heat into Washington, D.C. It was a dramatic demonstration of dissatisfaction with the status quo. Called the March on Washington for Jobs and Freedom, the event was organized through coordination by several civil rights groups. In the capital, in front of the Lincoln Memorial that day, Martin Luther King, Jr., gave his now famous "I have a dream . . ." speech, in which he eloquently exhorted the people of the United States to see his vision of a time when people in America would be judged based on character, not color.

In 1965 King led a voter registration campaign in Alabama and led a freedom march from Selma to Montgomery. All of these activities were tinged with danger for all the participants—the times were charged with the ugly emotions of hatred and prejudice. Every march, every boycott was perceived by white southerners as another affront. But King and his followers believed in the righteousness—and the necessity—of this cause.

"This is no time to engage in the luxury of cooling off or to take the tranquilizing drug of gradualism," said King on August 28, 1963. "Now is the time to make real the promises of democracy. Now is the time to make justice a reality for all of God's children."

From Montgomery, King moved north. During 1966 he lived in Chicago, and there he tried to encourage African Americans to take on the housing segregation there—which, while not the law, was the practice. He also spent time in the Birmingham jail again in 1967 for a contempt of court violation connected with an earlier demonstration.

By now more dramatic, more militant and even violent civil rights organizations were beginning to form, competing for followers. King could see that the time was past when he could keep the lid on violence, however great his own commitment to nonviolent tactics. Other organizations, with differing agendas, began to gain strength, including Carmichael's SNCC; the Congress for Racial Equality (CORE); the Black Panther Party, founded in 1966 by Huey P. Newton and Bobby Seale; and the Black Muslims, led in part by Malcolm X, who also founded the secular Organization for Afro-American Unity.

In agreement with the antiwar sentiments of his wife, Coretta Scott King, he began in 1967 to speak out against the war in Vietnam. This step alienated him from many moderates among his followers because it distanced the black cause from friends in the Democratic Party who were supporting the war. But King had begun to see that issues he had once thought of as simple were more complex than he had made allowance for. Of keen intelligence and struggling to be pure in his purpose, he became willing to break with any old alliances that could hurt the cause of racial equality and justice.

King also had begun to come under criticism for his "hit-and-run" tactics. He engaged in high-handed, high-profile grandstanding, his critics said, while the rank and file had to stay behind in the trenches and take the consequences afterward. King had begun to be thoughtful about these issues, as well, and in 1967, he went to Memphis, Tennessee, to work with predominantly black sanitation workers in negotiations for better working conditions and fairer wages. Unlike some of his earlier strategies, he stayed in Memphis for several months to get into the problem in depth.

It was his last project. In the midst of trying to reshape his role in the civil rights movement and improve it, this eloquent and dedicated worker on behalf of freedom and equality was cut down, on April 4, 1968 by an assassin's bullet. He was only 39 years old.

On March 10, 1969 James Earl Ray, a white man, was apprehended in England and pleaded guilty to the murder. He received a sentence of 99 years in prison.

But King left his dream behind as a legacy. He projected a new sense of worth and dignity to African Americans and poor people of any color. His philosophy of nonviolent direct action and his strategies for social change through rational and nondestructive methods were groundbreaking. King—and his words and actions—set the conscience of this nation in motion as few people had ever succeeded in doing before. And his wisdom, his words, his actions, his commitment and his dreams all intertwined with the American experience.

His remains were returned to Auburn Avenue, where a tomb was built as a monument outside the Center for Non-Violent Social Change, which was also established in his memory.

A CLOSE-UP

BIRTHPLACE, GRAVESITE AND FAMILY CHURCH

Martin Luther King, Jr.'s, birthplace at 501 Auburn Avenue, NE, is an unpretentious frame house with a wide front porch and a shingled roof. Inside, the parlor contains a piano that put forth many a hymn during his childhood. King grew up within a family that was comfortable, confident and committed to social justice.

The gravesite of Martin Luther King, Jr., where thousands of visitors come each year to pay homage   (Courtesy of the Atlanta Convention & Visitors Bureau, © Kevin C. Rose)

MARTIN LUTHER KING, JR., NATIONAL HISTORIC SITE

The Ebenezer Baptist Church is not far away, just a couple of long blocks, at 407 Auburn Avenue, NE. There, standing in the sanctuary, you can almost hear King's voice ringing out from the pulpit. This place also is tinged with tragedy. Here, as she was playing the church organ, Martin Luther King's mother was shot and killed by an assassin in 1974. Like the African Meeting House of the 19th century, this church stands at the center of the turbulent history of civil rights and the African-American experience in this century.

King's gravesite is also part of the National Historic Site, and so is the Center for Non-Violent Social Change (449 Auburn Avenue, NE), a monument to the legacy he left for urgent, nonviolent change in our world.

PRESERVING IT FOR THE FUTURE

In 1977 the Martin Luther King, Jr., Historic District was designated as a National Landmark. In 1980 the U.S. Congress created the Martin Luther King, Jr., National Historic Site, established as a unit of the National Park System to commemorate King's leadership in the civil rights movement. Since that time the National Park Service has worked to restore many of the homes in the neighborhood to reflect the way the community appeared when young Martin Luther King was growing up there in the 1930s.

EXPLORING ◆ FURTHER

Books by Martin Luther King

King, Martin Luther, Jr. *Stride Toward Freedom.* New York: Harper & Row, 1958.

———. *Why We Can't Wait.* New York: Harper & Row, 1963.

————. *Strength to Love.* New York: Harper & Row, 1963.

————. *Where Do We Go from Here: Chaos or Community?* New York: Harper & Row, 1967.

————. *The Trumpet of Conscience.* New York: Harper & Row, 1967.

Readings on Martin Luther King

Caldwell, Earl. "50,000 March in Capital to Support Demand by Poor for Sharing of Affluence." *New York Times*, June 20, 1968.

Davidson, Margaret. *I Have a Dream: The Story of Martin Luther King.* New York: Scholastic Paperbacks, 1994.

"Dr. King Is Honored." *New York Times*, July, 12 1977.

Garrow, David J. *Bearing the Cross: Martin Luther King, Jr., and the Southern Christian Leadership Conference.* New York: Morrow, 1986.

Haskins, Jim. *I Have a Dream: The Life and Words of Martin Luther King, Jr.* Brookfield, CT: Millbrook Press, 1992.

Lewis, David Levering. *King: A Critical Biography.* New York: Praeger, 1970.

Patterson, Lillie. *Martin Luther King, Jr. and the Freedom Movement.* Makers of America Series. New York: Facts On File, 1989.

Schulke, Flip. *He Had a Dream: Martin Luther King, Jr., and the Civil Rights Movement.* New York: W.W. Norton & Co., 1995.

Related Places:

APEX (African American Panoramic Experience) Museum
135 Auburn Avenue, NE
Atlanta, GA 30303
(404) 521-2739

Celebrates the local heritage of the Sweet Auburn area with audio-visual presentations, displays of artifacts and art exhibits, providing an informative introduction to the whole area.

The chapters of this book explore only a few of the hundreds of historic sites that commemorate black Americans and their contributions. Following is a partial list of additional historical places that reflect the varied African-American experience in the United States.

Northeastern States

Robert Gould Shaw and 54th Massachusetts Regiment Memorial
Boston Common
Boston, MA 02133
Memorial to soldiers of the all-black 54th Massachusetts Regiment, who fought on the Union side in the Civil War under the command of Robert Gould Shaw, white abolitionist. Sculpted by artist Augustus Saint Gaudens, this monument is a powerful tribute to this courageous group of soldiers and their contribution.

Memorial to Black Soldiers of the Battle of Rhode Island, 1778
Patriots Park
Route 114 at Route 24
Portsmouth, RI 02871
This monument commemorates the courage of the soldiers of the black regiment—composed of both free blacks and former slaves—who fought here on America's side in the Revolutionary War. After this battle, the black regiment fought in subsequent encounters, and in May 1781 all 40 of the regiment's men gave their lives in battle for America's cause at Points Bridge near Croton, New York.

John Dickinson Plantation
Kitts Hummock Road
P.O. Box 273
Dover, DE 19901
(301) 739-3277

This plantation dates back to the pre-Revolutionary 18th century and was inherited by John Dickinson in 1760. Influenced by Quaker beliefs in equal rights, he freed the slaves on his property, but many stayed to work for him. Today, visitors can tour the mansion built by Dickinson's father in 1740, as well as reconstructed log dwellings typical of the homes of most who worked the plantation—slaves, freed blacks or white. Both black and white interpreters can be seen on the grounds in period dress, and a special-focus tour, "A World Apart," focuses on the African-American experience on the plantation.

Southeastern States

Rosa Parks Historical Marker
One Court Square
Montgomery, AL 36104

This site, where slaves were once auctioned, marks the spot where, on December 1, 1955, Rosa Parks refused to comply with segregation by refusing to give up her seat to a white passenger on a Montgomery city bus.

Harper's Ferry National Historical Park
P.O. Box 65
Harpers Ferry, WV 25425
(304) 535-6371

The site of John Brown's famous 1859 raid, an ill-fated abolitionist insurrection intended to foment an anti-slavery revolution. The attack on the federal armory at Harper's Ferry failed, however, and most of John Brown's band, including the leader, were captured and hanged. The decision by Southern states to secede from the Union shortly thereafter was partially a reaction to Brown's provocative action and the great unrest it represented. Harpers Ferry was also the site, until the 1950s, of Storer College, an early normal school for freed African Americans. Black history is one of the interpretative themes of the park.

Zora Neale Hurston Museum of Art
227 East Kennedy Boulevard
P.O. Box 2586
Eatonville, FL 32751
(407) 647-3307

This museum and nearby Zora Neale Hurston Memorial Park and Marker (11 People Street) commemorate the life and work of writer and folklorist Hurston, who was born and raised in this town, the first incorporated all-black town in the United States. She later returned to Eatonville, where she wrote and set much of her fiction. Hurston's anthropological studies of her racial heritage influenced many Harlem Renaissance writers of the 1930s, as well as later writers, including Ralph Ellison, Alice Walker and Toni Morrison.

Midwestern States

Malcolm X Home Historical Markers
3448 Pinkney Street
Omaha, NE 68111

Two historical markers commemorate sites in Omaha where life began for Malcolm X, the 20th century's leading exponent of African-American self-reliance and the black nationalist movement. One marker was erected here by the state of Nebraska and the second by the black community.

Malcolm X Homesite Historical Marker
4705 South Logan Street
Lansing, MI 48910

A historical marker commemorates the site where Malcolm Little's family lived during the formative years of the man who would become Malcolm X.

Paul Lawrence Dunbar House
219 North Summit Avenue
Dayton, OH 45407
(513) 224-7061

Purchased with proceeds from Dunbar's poetry, this house was his home during the final years of his life until his untimely death in 1906 at 34, by which time his renown was widespread. In 1924 he was voted one of the ten greatest African Americans by a poll of the American Federation of Negro Students, although more recently he has been criticized for his reliance on dialect to convey African-American themes. Visitors find his home much as he left it—including his desk, typewriter, books and belongings, including a bicycle given him by his friends the Wright brothers and a ceremonial sword presented him by President Theodore Roosevelt.

Scott Joplin State Historic Site
2658 Delmar Blvd.
St. Louis, MO 63013
(314) 533-1003

Musician Scott Joplin had the entire nation tapping its toes with his ragtime compositions and was already famous for his "Maple Leaf Rag" by the time he moved in 1900 with his bride, Belle Hayden, to 2658A Morgan Street (now Delmar Boulevard). The three years he lived here were among the most productive of his tragically short life and he wrote some of his most famous compositions here, including "March Majestic," "Ragtime Dance," "Elite Syncopation" and "The Entertainer."

Central High School
1500 Park Street
Little Rock, AR 72202
(501) 376-4751

Prior to 1957, Little Rock's Central High School was segregated. But in the fall of that year, nine black students began attending school there, amid threats from opposing white mobs. Arkansas's governor used the state's National Guard to block the black teenagers from approaching the school grounds, but a federal court finally ordered removal of the troops and local police escorted the students to school. However, the mood of the crowd became dangerous, and finally the situation was resolved when President Dwight D. Eisenhower federalized the Arkansas National Guard and sent in federal paratroopers. The children finally did establish their right to integrate the school, protected by federal troops carrying bayonets and by the Supreme Court's three-year-old *Brown* v. *Board of Education* decision that public school segregation was unconstitutional. A marker on the school grounds recalls these historic events.

George Washington Carver National Monument
P.O. Box 38
Diamond, MO 64840
(417) 325-4151

Located near Joplin, the boyhood home of scientist George Washington Carver commemorates his early years spent in slavery. Visitors can see the site of the log cabin (partially reconstructed), where Carver was born, as well as the house his father later built, and can walk the trails through the woods, where the future botanist and agronomist first developed his understanding of nature. As a child he was locally known as the "plant doctor," and as an adult he developed more than 300 uses for peanuts and more than 100 uses for sweet potatoes.

Southwestern States

Fort Davis National Historic Site
Highways 17 and 118
Fort Davis, TX 79734
(915) 426-3225

Fort Davis, in west Texas, lay between Mescalero Apache territory and the "Great Comanche War Trail," and after Confederate soldiers abandoned the fort in 1862, it was destroyed by Apaches who rightly saw it as a threat. Four years later, four companies of the 9th Cavalry, one of two newly formed black regiments, arrived and began rebuilding Fort Davis. The 9th Cavalry, as well as three other groups of the black soldiers of the

West known as Buffalo Soldiers—the 10th Cavalry and the 24th and 25th Infantry—spent time at Fort Davis and the surrounding desert countryside that was threatened by Apache and Comanche warriors. Visitors to Fort Davis can view interpretative displays that commemorate these soldiers, as well as a diorama and slide show that include information about their role here.

Western States

Black American West Museum
3091 California Street
Denver, CO 80205
(303) 292-2566

This museum celebrates the presence of African Americans in the Old West, including Dr. Justina Ford, who settled in Denver in 1902 and, over the course of the next 50 years, delivered more than 7,000 children. Ford lived in the home that is the present site of the museum that commemorates her life, as well as the wide range of the African-American contributions of every kind to the culture of the West. There photographs and artifacts of the time conjure up a picture of daily life—for black ranch hands, miners, homesteaders, soldiers, and many others, including the sharpshooter named Nat Love, also known as "Deadwood Dick."

Henderson House Museum
602 DesChutes Way
Tumwater, WA 98501
(360) 754-4120

George Bush, whose father was a black sailor and whose mother was an Irish housemaid, helped settle this area in the 1840 with a party headed by Michael Simmons. Bush figured prominently in the transformation of the territory now known as Washington into a state. He is honored at the Henderson House Museum with a permanent display, and he is listed with other founders of the town of Tumwater, Washington, on the memorial located in Tumwater Falls Historical Park at the foot of Grant Street. He and his wife, Isabella Bush, are buried with others of the original exploratory party in the Tumwater Pioneer Cemetery on Little Rock Road in Tumwater.

Pima Air & Space Museum
6000 East Valencia Road
Tucson, AZ 85706
(602) 574-0646

Among the highlights at this museum is an exhibit celebrating the career of African-American pilot Janet Harmon Bragg, born in Georgia, whose pioneer piloting in the 1930s broke barriers both for African Americans and for women. Among aircraft displays and numerous presentations on other topics, additional exhibits here center on the all-black Tuskegee Airmen; on Captain Lloyd "Fig" Newton, who was the first African American to fly as a member of the Thunderbirds, the Air Force's acrobatic flying team; and on the black contribution to America's space program.

MORE READING SOURCES

In addition to the suggested readings at the end of each chapter of this book, the following list provides additional suggestions for exploring further.

Allen, James S. Reconstruction—The Battle for Democracy. New York: International Publishers, 1937.

Burchard, Peter. "We'll Stand by the Union"; Robert Gould Shaw and the Black 54th Massachusetts Regiment. Facts On File, 1993.

Carmichael, Stokely, and Charles V. Hamilton. Black Power. New York: Knopf, Inc., 1967.

Christian, Charles M. Black Saga: The African American Experience, A Chronology. With the assistance of Sari J. Bennett, Boston: Houghton Mifflin Co., 1995.

Chase, Henry. In Their Footsteps. The American Visions Guide to African-American Heritage Sites. New York: Henry Holt and Co., 1994.

Cleaver, Eldridge. Soul On Ice. New York: McGraw-Hill, 1968.

Daniel, Peter. Shadow of Slavery: Peonage in the South. New York: Oxford University Press, 1972.

Davidson, Basil. The African Slave Trade. Boston-Toronto: Little, Brown and Co., 1961.

Dennis, Denise. Black History for Beginners, illustrated by Susan Willmarth. New York: Writers and Readers Publishing, Inc., 1995.

Estell, Kenneth. African America: Portrait of a People. Detroit: Visible Ink, 1994.

Golay, Michael. Reconstruction and Reaction: The Black Experience of

Emancipation, 1861–1913. Library of African American History. New York: Facts On File, 1996.

Gutman, Herbert G. *The Black Family in Slavery and Freedom.* New York: Random House, 1976.

Haley, Alex and Malcolm X. *The Autobiography of Malcolm X.* New York: Grove Press, 1965.

Huggins, Nathan Irvin. *Voices from the Harlem Renaissance.* New York: Oxford University Press, 1976.

Loewenberg, James and Ruth Bogin. *Black Women in 19th Century American Life.* University Park and London: Pennsylvania State University Press, 1976.

Lewis, David Levering. *When Harlem Was in Vogue.* New York: Oxford University Press, 1989.

Morrison-Reed, Mark D. *Black Pioneers.* Boston: Beacon Press, 1980.

Scott, John Anthony, and Robert Alan Scott. *John Brown of Harper's Ferry.* New York: Facts On File, 1988.

Smith, Jessie Carney. *Epic Lives: One Hundred Black Women Who Made a Difference.* Detroit: Visible Ink Press, 1993.

Wepman, Dennis. *The Struggle for Freedom: African-American Slave Resistance.* Library of African-American History. New York: Facts On File, 1996.

INDEX